★ FOREWORD TO THIS 2ND

Welcome to the 'expanded' 2005 Second Edition of my book; rep
in 2011! What's new and 'expanded' about it, you ask? Well, apart
and additions here and there, the most important addition is 40 brand new **'PUPIL'S ACTIVITY SHEETS'** in the last section of the book (39 added in 2005, and 1 more added in 2011). This actually increases the size of the original first edition of the book by almost half again!

But why did I include these new pages, you now wonder? Well, firstly they illustrate all 40 of the experiments described in one way or another within the 24 sections of the original edition of the book, which is now the first two-thirds of this book! Secondly, these **PUPIL'S ACTIVITY SHEETS** are so called because they are just perfect for copying and giving to pupils to work from. You will see that each pupil's sheet contains just the basic instructions on how to do each experiment mentioned in the first main body of the book:

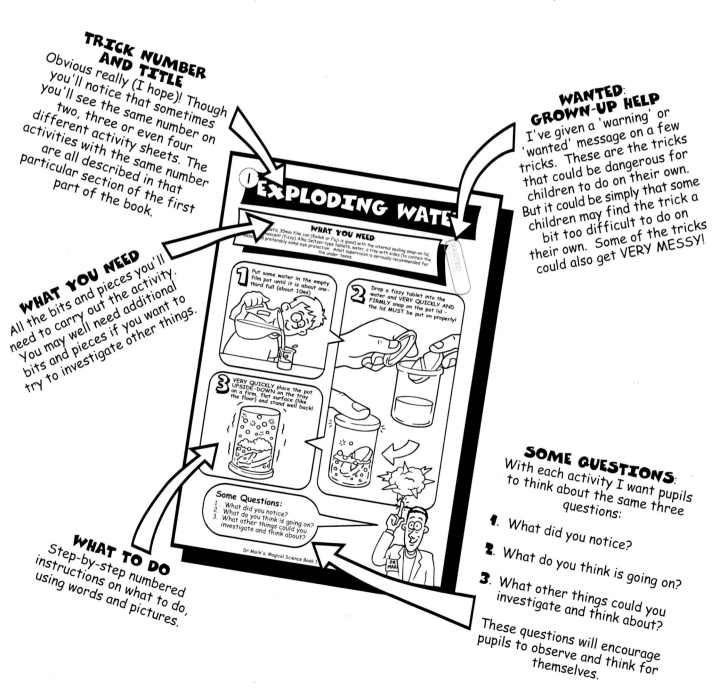

TRICK NUMBER AND TITLE
Obvious really (I hope)! Though you'll notice that sometimes you'll see the same number on two, three or even four different activity sheets. The activities with the same number are all described in that particular section of the first part of the book.

WHAT YOU NEED
All the bits and pieces you'll need to carry out the activity. You may well need additional bits and pieces if you want to try to investigate other things.

WHAT TO DO
Step-by-step numbered instructions on what to do, using words and pictures.

WANTED: GROWN-UP HELP
I've given a 'warning' or 'wanted' message on a few tricks. These are the tricks that could be dangerous for children to do on their own. But it could be simply that some children may find the trick a bit too difficult to do on their own. Some of the tricks could also get VERY MESSY!

SOME QUESTIONS:
With each activity I want pupils to think about the same three questions:

1. What did you notice?
2. What do you think is going on?
3. What other things could you investigate and think about?

These questions will encourage pupils to observe and think for themselves.

© Dr Mark Biddiss 2001, 2005, 2011, Magical Science Book 1 @ www.Dr-Mark.co.uk

A SET OF FUN & NOVEL EXPERIMENTS ABOUT PHYSICAL PROCESSES, PROPERTIES OF MATERIALS & OURSELVES

Written by

'Dr Mark' Biddiss
of Dr Mark's INPIREeducation™, INSPIREscience™ & INSPIREmaths™

Graphic Design & Illustrated by
Jeff Parker

Published by Dr Mark's INSPIREducation, 2011

© Dr Mark Biddiss 2001, 2005, 2011, Magical Science Book 1 @ www.Dr-Mark.co.uk

I re-dedicate this book to the very special children, all of whom were my friends, formerly at the now sadly closed Thurlow Park Special Needs School in, LONDON, UK
- with whom it was an honour and privilege to work.

And especially to my own son, Sebastian.

About Dr Mark - The Author

'Dr Mark' Biddiss - formerly a gas-man turned space-scientist and college lecturer - is now a science and maths educational provider, teacher trainer and writer. He is a member of the Society of Education Consultants and the Society of Authors. Since 1996, he has specialised in researching and designing science and maths activities to engage and inspire people about science and maths, and the thinking skills involved.

Since 1997 'Dr Mark' has visited many hundreds of schools all over the UK with his lively and fun science and maths pupil shows, hands-on pupil workshops and teacher training days. He has worked directly with countless thousands of pupils - aged 4 to 16 - and their teachers, delivering to ALL abilities, including Special Needs, more able, Gifted & Talented pupils.

'Dr Mark' is widely regarded as a popular and inspirational speaker and educational provider, and is engaged regularly by many high-profile clients, including numerous local government authorities around the UK. He is also called upon regularly to speak at national annual teacher conference events, including the TES Teaching Conferences and the NEC Education Show.

'Dr Mark' currently divides his professional time between working directly with pupils, teacher training, conference presentations, further research into 'Advanced Thinking & Learning' and writing teachers' books and resources.

His other titles, most available as printed books, e-books, CDROMs and in DVD format, are:

Dr Mark's Magical Science 1
Dr Mark's Magical Science 2
Dr Mark's Magical Maths 1
Dr Mark's Magical Maths 2
Dr Mark's Circus Science
Dr Mark's Sound of Science
Dr Mark's Explosive Experiments
Dr Mark's Mathemagic & Arithmetricks

For further details about Dr Mark's products and services, see his website:
www.Dr-Mark.co.uk

About Jeff - The Graphic Designer & Illustrator

Jeff Parker has been working in design & illustration forover twenty years
with a client list as diverse as the styles in which he works.
To receive some samples of his work or to discuss a project please contact him on-
01462 678828 or 07881 760582
or email- jeffparkerillustration@hotmail.com

BOOK 1 CONTENTS

	Page No.
An Introduction	5
So who is this book for?	6
Using this book	7

      Fair Testing
      If you are a teacher
      If you are a parent
      If you are a child

Science Trick Layout – how each experiment is written out	9
Safety! Safety! Safety! & WANTED: GROWN-UP HELP	11

Dr Mark's Magical Science Experiments

1. **Exploding Water**   12/86
   An experiment that explores the chemical reaction between the sodium bicarbonate and other substances in effervescent tablets (such as 'Alka Seltzer') and water, inside a sealed film canister, resulting in a surprisingly 'forceful' explosion.

2. **Levitating Balloons & Floating Balls**   15/87
   Two experiments that explore the effects of an up-thrusting air-stream, from blowing through a drinking straw and from a blow hair-dryer, on different size balloons and ping-pong balls.

3. **Losing Control**   18/89
   An experiment that explores the importance of your vision in your sense of balance.

4. **'Orrible Ooze**   21/90
   An experiment that explores the surprising liquid-solid properties of mixing water with cornflower (or cornstarch) or custard powder.

5. **Screaming Straws & Raspberry Balloons**   24/91
   Two experiments that explore the noisy effects of blowing air through a specially cut milk-shake drinking straw or long balloon.

6. **Phantom Pencils**   27/93
   An experiment that explores how sensitive and insensitive your skin is on different parts of your body.

7. **Black Magic & Secret Colours**   30/94
   Two experiments that explore the effects of capillary action in the chromatography of separating the colours that make up black ink and the coloured dye used on candy-sweets.

8. **Diving Pen-tops & Orange Peel, and Saucy Sinker**   33/96
   Three experiments that explore 'floating and sinking' in buoyancy, and the compression properties if liquids (water) and gases (air).

9. **Holey Hands**   36/99
   An experiment that explores how your brain combines the images it sees from each eye and how very different images from each eye can cause you to see some surprising things!

10. **Bag Bombs & Self-Inflating Balloons**   39/100
    Two experiments that explore the chemical reaction between sodium bicarbonate (baking soda) and vinegar, and how it can be used to 'explode' a zip-lock bags and inflate a balloon.

11.   Obedient Squirty Bottle   42/102
An experiment that explores the surprising effects of air pressure in stopping water from squirting from the wide open holes in a plastic bottle and the effects of pressure from your hands in squirting the water through the same holes.

12.   Magnetic Hands & Weightless Arms   45/103
Two experiments that explore how your muscles can sometimes 'mysteriously' make your hands feel as if they are repelling each other and make your outstretched arms 'float' upwards on their own.

13.   Fire Raising & Sucking Glasses   48/105
Two experiments that explore the 'suction effect' of cooling, contracting warm air on lifting water inside a glass.

14.   Mystery of the Moving Egg Eggsperiment   51/107
A novel and engaging experiment which explores the forces and motion effects of the liquid inside a raw egg and the solid inside a hard-boiled egg, and how this can help you tell the difference between the two.

15.   Tasteless Tongue & Apple Potatoes   54/108
Two experiments that explore how your sense of taste sometimes can't tell the difference between different foods and sometimes gets it totally wrong! They also demonstrate how your senses of smell and taste work together to give you your 'sense' of flavour.

16.   Bouncin' Blubber Balls   57/110
An experiment that explores the surprising bouncy properties of a material made from squirting PVA white glue into a borax solution.

17.   Balloon Kebabs & Water-Bag Porcupines   60/111
Two experiments that explore the surprising properties of balloon rubber and polythene plastic bags which allow you to push a sharp stick right through without popping either.

18.   White Ghosts & Spectral Spectres   63/114
Two experiments that explore how you see colours and how when you tire out your eyes you see 'ghostly' things that aren't really there!

19.   Soapy Speed-Boats, Floating Metal, Scary Finger & Petrified Pepper, and Water Circle   66/116
Four experiments that explore the surprising surface tension properties of water and detergent in making things move, and how the surface of water can even support metal!

20.   Flying Flipping Fish   69/120
An experiment that explores the surprising aerodynamic flying properties of a simple strip of paper easily cut and folded into a fish-shape.

21.   Colour-Names & Naming Colours   72/121
An experiment that explores how your ability to read words and name colours can become totally confused!

22.   Crushing Cans & Ghostly Shrinking Bottles   78/122
Two experiments that explore the surprising 'crushing' properties of air pressure on tin cans and plastic bottles.

23.   Unreadable Words & Invisible Letters   78/124
Two experiments that explore how you sometimes seem to completely fail to notice words and letters right in front of your eyes!

24.   Vanishing Rings & Linking Loops   81/125
A set of surprising, 'brain-twisting' paper-cutting investigations about the classic, novel and engaging 'Moebius' strip or loop, and its use in science.

SCIENCE TOPIC-BASED TABLE OF EXPERIMENTS   82/83

NOTES (blank for you to write on)   126/127

DR MARK'S BOOKS   128

AN INTRODUCTION

HELLO! - and well done for looking into this book! But I must start with a **WARNING:** by reading from this book you are in very, very serious risk of getting hooked into the amazing and wonderful universe of science!

We all live in an exciting and fascinating universe - in case you haven't noticed! But I like to show people just how much fun the universe can be too and how much fun they can have with it! Not only that, I also want to show how so very often science and the universe can seem to be very magical, strange, amazing, weird, mysterious, perplexing, wacky, and down right curious!

As a trained scientist myself, I also want to share with people what it feels like to be a scientist. That is one of the big reasons why I decided to write this first book.

From what I can see, I think that we are all born as 'scientists' (and 'artists' too). I got some of my 'evidence' and 'conclusions' about this by watching my son, Sebastian, playing and exploring the world around him from when he was a baby. He did everything that grown-up scientists do! He would think a lot about the 'problem', look and examine things very carefully, ask questions and try out ideas. He would repeat the same 'experiment' with his toys (or the box it came in) over and over again, and also change things to see what happens. From all this he would work out new things about the world around him. And finally he would tell everyone all about it! This is pretty much the so called 'scientific process' that scientists use! I have also seen scientists stamp their feet, bang their fists, laugh, cry, stick their tongue out while thinking and dribble too, by the way - including me!

But why are tiny children so good at being scientists I wondered? I decided that at least one of the reasons must simply be because they find the things they are 'exploring' to be really interesting and 'enjoyable' in some way, and so they want to try to learn all about them. So I had a thought, "How can I help older children and grown-ups to find the things they are 'exploring' to be really interesting and 'enjoyable' in some way as well, and so want to learn all about them too?" And then I thought, "I know, I'll show them all the magical science 'tricks' that I know."

You see, children simply love magic tricks (as do most adults for that matter!). The reason most people love magic tricks is because something mysterious appears to happen which they can't easily explain. Many of the magic tricks we have seen, such as sawing people in half and making people or objects appear and disappear, are those we have seen on television or on the stage. These tricks usually involve illusion, props, slight-of-hand and pre-arranged stage management. However, you can easily perform dozens of simple, fun science experiments and demonstrations which can also appear to be magical or mysterious in some way. The fact that they have a magical and mysterious appearance makes them really interesting to many people. And these people are normally very keen and willing to learn how and why the tricks work.

So I thought that I could use and 'exploit' this interest and eagerness, to show my 'audience' the science principles behind the tricks. In fact, as you will soon discover, the magical science 'tricks' in this book can form the basis for an entire science investigation. HAVE FUN!

JUST WHO IS THIS BOOK FOR?

ARE YOU A TEACHER?
Then this book is for you!
You will find it a great resource for fun science demonstrations and investigations for the classroom or home. I guarantee that the science magic 'tricks' in this book will liven-up your science lessons and enthuse your pupils about science. Your pupils will also think that you are the best science teacher ever!

ARE YOU A CHILD?
Then this book is for you!
It is full of fun and amazing science magic tricks you can do yourself. Though you will have a lot more fun doing the activities with friends and grown-ups around. You will be able to impress them with just how amazingly clever you are with science and how much fun it can all be!

ARE YOU A PARENT?
Then this book is for you!
You and your family can have hours of quality time having fun exploring the magic of science together. Or learn the tricks yourself and impress your offspring with your amazing scientific knowledge!

ARE YOU A SCIENCE LECTURER IN COLLEGE OR A UNIVERSITY WITH OLDER STUDENTS
Then this book is for you!
I have used many scientific novelties, curiosities and tricks, including those in this book, to see just how much the students really understand about science, by asking them to explain to me what's going on. I know you can do the same too!

ARE YOU ANY OTHER SORT OF ADULT?
Then this book is for you!
You don't need children or students as an excuse to have some fun with the science tricks in my book - if you need an excuse then pretend that you are learning the tricks to impress your friends at parties!

In fact
THIS BOOK IS FOR ANYONE AND EVERYONE!

© Dr Mark Biddiss 2001, 2005, 2011, Magical Science Book 1 @ www.Dr-Mark.co.uk

USING THIS BOOK

Like many books, this one is divided into different parts. These different parts are listed in the 'BOOK 1 CONTENTS' pages. I strongly suggest you make sure that you know what is written there. You will discover that the book is divided into two main sections. The first main section contains full written details of all the 40 experiments featured in the book, written in 24 experiment chapters. The second main section of the book contains the illustrated pupil worksheets for the described experiments.

Turn this page over and next you will find the 'SCIENCE TRICK LAYOUT' pages. As the title suggests, these two pages show you just how each and every science trick in the book is written and drawn out. These pages are important to anyone using this book.

As you will see, this is a 'doing' science book. Doing the science tricks will give you the best learning experience and the most fun! Once you have all the bits and pieces in front of you, doing any of the tricks will only take a few minutes. But if you want to explore further you are going to need about 30 minutes to an hour.

FAIR TESTING

If you do a trick and then want to change something to see or 'test' what happens, you need to make sure that you do a 'fair test'. The main idea of fair testing is that if you want to change something to see what happens, you should only change that one thing at a time, leaving everything else the same and unchanged. An important reason for this can be put as a question. If you change more than one thing at the same time, and something different happens with the experiment, how will you know what caused the difference? It may be because you changed one thing, or another thing, or maybe because you changed two things at the same time! And it gets a lot more complicated if you change three or more things at the same time! So, by changing only one thing at a time and keeping everything else the same, if something different does happen, you have a pretty good clue as to why. It's most likely because you changed that one thing, and changing that one thing caused something different to happen! Fair enough?

IF YOU ARE A TEACHER

There are one or two particular features of the book I would like to bring to your attention.

Firstly, and if you have not realised this already, you will find this book to be a great resource of fun and magical science demonstrations and experiments which will definitely 'liven-up' your science lessons.

About a third of the science tricks are mainly to do with Physics: Physical Processes, about a third to do with Chemistry: Properties of Materials, and about a third to do with Biology: Living Things, 'ourselves' in particular. The more obvious or stronger topic links of each trick are listed in the 'SOME OF THE SCIENCE YOU'RE EXPLORING' box, on the first page of each experiment. You will find a more detailed list of links in the 'SCIENCE TOPIC-BASED TABLE OF EXPERIMENTS' spread on pages 84 and 85 near the back of the book.

Looking at these two pages you will notice straight away that most of the tricks actually have links with more than one main science topic. Some of the links are not so obvious, but they are there nonetheless. For example, 'EXPLODING WATER' not only has strong links with both Chemistry and Physics, but also has some links with Biology (digestion) as well. This is certainly not unusual in 'everyday' science. And it can be extremely useful to the science teacher who wants to illustrate more than one science topic with the same science trick. One way of using this table is to see if the science topic you plan to cover with your pupils is listed. If it is, you can then see how many of the science tricks in the book are related in some way to this topic. Then simply choose the one or more you like the best to show or do with your pupils.

 © Dr Mark Biddiss 2001, 2005, 2011, Magical Science Book 1 @ www.Dr-Mark.co.uk

Also, remember that I am happy for you to photocopy pages from the book for your pupils. The first 'instructions' page of each science trick would be good to give to your pupils to do the experiment from, either at home or in class.

I decided to have the book 'wire bound' because it will make it easier to keep the book open flat on the table top or on the photocopying machine, without damaging the spine of the book by squashing it flat.

IF YOU ARE A PARENT

As a parent, you have a very important role to play when using this book with your child. Most importantly, you can help them to get the most out of each experiment by helping them when and where they need help. But try not to help too much. Encourage your child to do and think for themselves as much as they can. If you feel the need, read right through the trick first yourself before you do the experiment with your child. This will show you what I want them to do and to think about. However, another way in which you can really share the exploration experience would be to do the experiment with them, step by step, without reading through yourself first. Many children enjoy and benefit greatly from 'sharing' like this with their parents. And don't worry too much if you get things wrong or make mistakes; if you handle this right your children will quite likely respect you all the more for it and 'making mistakes' is all part of the fun of experimental science anyway!

In any event, you will be able to have hours of fun with your child exploring the magic in science! Not only that, you will be helping them to gain a better appreciation of the amazing world around them and help them with their science studies at school as well!

IF YOU ARE A CHILD

Most importantly, I want you to HAVE FUN with this book! You will have the most fun if you follow my instructions properly. Remember, you will need to have a grown-up to help you with some of my science tricks - especially the more dangerous or difficult ones. You may also need a grown-up to help you understand what I want you to do. But believe it or not, having a grown-up around can be lots of fun! For one thing, you are going to need a 'friend' to do some of the tricks on. Grown-ups make great 'friends'! Grown-ups are also really good at getting all the things you need and at cleaning up after you! Though I would say that good science explorers often try to do all of this for themselves when they can.

The next two pages will show you how each science trick is written out. You may want to do a trick on your own, and my not need grown-up help. If so, then try to read only the parts of the trick layout you need. To do the trick you only need to read the first 'instruction' page and the 'SOME TRICK TIPS' box on the third page. Working through the questions is the best way of learning and having fun. But don't cheat and read the answers before you try the questions yourself first! Scientists should never cheat!

Anyway, as I said, most importantly **HAVE FUN!**

SCIENCE TRICK LAYOUT
(How each experiment is written out)

I've grouped the 40 experiment 'tricks' in this book into 24 sections. Each section starts with the 'main' activity on the first page, and in most sections has details of one or more 'associated' activities. You also have 40 illustrated activity sheets in total, all grouped together in the second 'PUPIL'S ACTIVITY SHEETS' part of the book. I have written each of the 24 grouped sections under the same ten headed sub-sections, spread over three pages. The headings are:

1. OBJECTIVE
2. WHAT YOU NEED
3. SOME OF THE SCIENCE YOU'RE EXPLORING
4. WHAT TO DO ILLUSTRATED INSTRUCTIONS
5. WHAT HAPPENS
6. SOME QUESTIONS TO THINK ABOUT
7. SO WHAT'S GOING ON?
8. WHERE ON EARTH?
9. SOME TRICK TIPS
10. ANSWERS TO SOME OF THE NUMBERED QUESTIONS

Here's how it all works:

FIRST PAGE -
the 'what you need' and 'what to do' instructions page:

NOTE: If you want to have a go at the science trick without knowing what happens first, then this is the only whole page you really need to look at to start with. This is the instruction page you could photocopy for others to do the experiment from. However, you (and them) will also need to know what I've written in the **'SOME TRICK TIPS'** box on the third page of each trick.

TRICK NUMBER AND TITLE
(obvious really!)

OBJECTIVE
What I want you to try and do.

WHAT YOU NEED
All the bits you'll need if you want to have a go at everything. In many of the tricks I've suggested two or three things you can try. If you only want to try one or two, then you may not need everything listed. I suggest that you read through the instructions first to see.

WHAT TO DO
Step-by-step numbered instructions on what to do, using words and pictures.

WANTED: GROWN-UP HELP
I've given a 'warning' or 'wanted' message on a few tricks. These are the tricks that could be dangerous for children to do on their own. But it could be simply that some children may find the trick a bit too difficult to do on their own. Some of the tricks could also get VERY MESSY!

SOME OF THE SCIENCE YOU'RE EXPLORING
With each trick for your interest I've included a short list of the main science topics you'll be investigating. I've included a more detailed and complete **'TOPIC-BASED INDEX'** towards the end of the book on pages 84 and 85. This lists the more obvious links of each trick to the main branches of science. These are the science topics that children learn about at school.

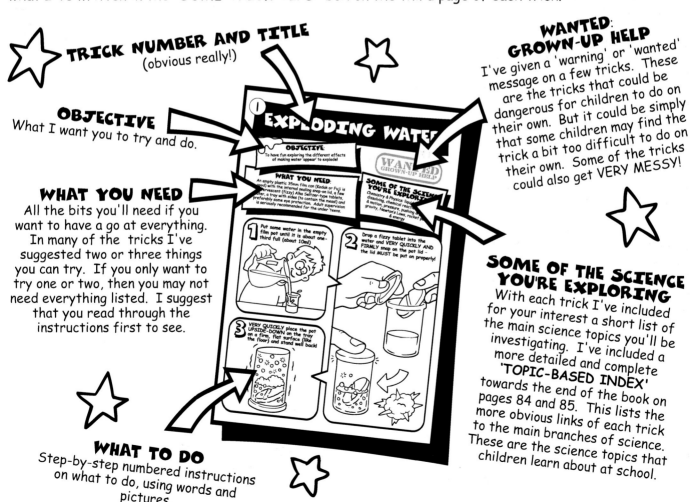

© Dr Mark Biddiss 2001, 2005, 2011, Magical Science Book 1 @ www.Dr-Mark.co.uk

SECOND PAGE -
the 'what happens', 'questions' and 'what's going on' page:

WHAT HAPPENS?
What you should see happen if all goes to plan.

SOME QUESTIONS TO THINK ABOUT
A list of questions to think about including 'What do you think is going on?' and 'What other things could you try and change?'

SO WHAT'S GOING ON
Here I've given the scientific explanation of what happens and why. I've tried to avoid using any unnecessary scientific 'jargon'. I've also tried not to assume too much about what you know of science already.

THIRD PAGE -
the 'where on Earth', 'trick tips' and 'answers to questions' page:

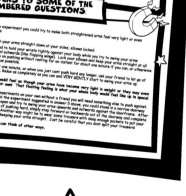

WHERE ON EARTH?
Here I've described one or two examples of things going on in the world which work and can be explained using the same or similar scientific ideas as your science trick.

SOME TRICK TIPS
A few suggestions, ideas and tips which should help you to get your science trick to work properly and well, and to warn you of any possible hazards and safety concerns, or other problems you need to be aware of.

ANSWERS TO SOME OF THE NUMBERED QUESTIONS
I won't usually give you the answers and explanations to ALL of my questions. The ones I leave out are usually easy enough for you to experiment with and get the answer for yourself.

© Dr Mark Biddiss 2001, 2005, 2011, Magical Science Book 1 @ www.Dr-Mark.co.uk

SAFETY! SAFETY! SAFETY! & WANTED: GROWN-UP HELP

SAFETY is something all scientists, young or old, need to think about all the time. But let me say right from the start that most of the experiments are safe enough for children to do without any grown-up help. In fact, only three NEED grown-up supervision throughout. But grown-ups may be needed for some of the experiments for other reasons.

I usually say early on in the experiment if I think grown-up help is needed. Quite often I use the message, 'WANTED: GROWN-UP HELP'. If I do write this, it is because I do not think that a child should do this experiment without a grown-up nearby. But this may not always be because the experiment is particularly dangerous in an obvious way.

Instead, it may be because a grown-up needs to help prepare something for the child to do, such as boil an egg for the 'Mystery of the Moving Egg' eggsperiment, or make some holes in a plastic bottle with a pin or nail in the 'Obedient squirty Bottle' trick.

A grown-up may want to be around for one or two activities which use materials which could be used in an unsafe way. One example of this would be the 'Bouncin' Blubber Balls & Potty Putty' experiment. In this experiment you will need to use borax and PVA white glue. Neither of these substances are poisonous in themselves, but they could still make you ill if you ate them.

Sometimes a grown-up needs to be around because the experiment would be too difficult for a young child to do on their own or which could get very messy without a little grown-up help!

Maybe a grown-up will even need to be around to protect children from other grown-ups because one or two of the experiments may be very irritating or annoying to others! I'm thinking of the 'Screaming Straws & Raspberry Balloons' experiments in particular!

Lastly, a grown-up may be needed because they are actually part of the experiment themselves! Two experiments come to mind here, but I'll let you find out which ones they are and what the grown-up is needed for!

You should also read **'SOME TRICK TIPS'** on the third page of each experiment. Here I mention any other hazards or safety concerns about that particular trick that you may not have thought about and which may not be clear and obvious from the start. Remember: so called 'common sense' isn't as common as it should be, particularly when people are having a good time!

So please, just....
BE SENSIBLE AND BE SAFE!

① EXPLODING WATER

OBJECTIVE: To have fun exploring the different effects of making water 'appear' to explode!

WANTED GROWN-UP HELP

WHAT YOU NEED: An empty plastic 35mm film can (Kodak or Fuji is good) with the internal sealing snap-on lid, a few effervescent (fizzy) Alka Seltzer-type tablets, water, a tray with sides (to contain the mess!) and preferably some eye protection. Adult supervision is seriously recommended for the under 'teens.

SOME OF THE SCIENCE YOU'RE EXPLORING: Chemistry & Physics: liquids & gases, dissolving, chemical reactions, forces & motion, pressure, pushing & pulling, gravity, Newton's Laws, rocket power & energy

1 Put some water in the empty film pot until it is about one-third full (about 10ml)

2 Drop a fizzy tablet into the water and VERY QUICKLY AND FIRMLY snap on the pot lid – the lid MUST be put on properly!

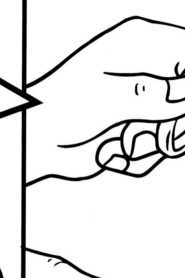

3 VERY QUICKLY place the pot UPSIDE-DOWN on the tray on a firm, flat surface (like the floor) and stand well back!

© Dr Mark Biddiss 2001, 2005, 2011, Magical Science Book 1 @ www.Dr-Mark.co.uk

WHAT HAPPENS?

After just a few seconds the film pot will explode high up into the air, leaving the lid on the floor!

SOME QUESTIONS TO THINK ABOUT

1. What do you think is going on? (see 'SO WHAT'S GOING ON?')
2. Why is it so important for the lid to be snapped onto the can firmly and fitted properly?
3. What happens if you keep the amount of water the same but change the amount of tablet, e.g., try a whole piece, then a half, then a quarter? (answer provided)
4. What happens if you keep the amount of water AND the amount of tablet the same, but change the number and size of pieces of tablet that you put into the can (see 'SOME TRICK TIPS' for an example)? (answer provided)
5. What happens if you keep the amount of water the same, the amount of tablet the same and the number of pieces of tablet the same, but change the temperature of the water, e.g., hand-hot, room temperature and freezing cold? (answer provided)
6. What happens if you keep all the above variables the same but change the type of liquid you use? (answer provided)
7. What other things could you change if you leave all the other above variables the same? (answer provided)

(numbered answers to most of the questions are given at the bottom of the next page)

SO WHAT'S GOING ON?

When a dry effervescent (fizzy) tablet is put into the water in the pot, a 'chemical reaction' takes place between the chemicals in the tablet and the water (the reacants). The tablet dissolves and releases gas (the product) in the chemical process (effervescent tablets usually release Carbon Dioxide gas). This gas bubbles up through the water and into the air space above. As more and more gas bubbles up into the space above, the pressure of the gas increases. For the pressurized gas to escape, it must first force the water down and out of the pot, because the water is in the way! Eventually the gas pressure builds up so much above the water that the lid of the pot can no longer grip and hold it in and so it is suddenly forced off and downwards, allowing the water and gas to escape. Since the gas, water and pot lid are all moving with force downwards, the empty pot is forced upwards. Eventually, gravity slows the upward moving pot down enough and pulls it back down again!

This experiment is a good example of Isaac Newton's Third Law of Motion that says that for every action there is an equal and opposite reaction. Effectively, the lid and the water are the driving agents with the compressed gas providing the energy.

WHERE ON EARTH?

Explosions owing to the build up of gas pressure like that in this experiment - are known to occur in volcanoes and at other volcanic sites. With some volcanic explosions the build up of gas pressure takes place over a long period of time, whereas with others the build up happens very quickly. Burping or belching, and farting are similarly caused by a build up of gas pressure in the body and its sudden release.

SOME TRICK TIPS!

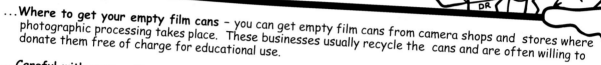

- ...**Where to get your empty film cans** – you can get empty film cans from camera shops and stores where photographic processing takes place. These businesses usually recycle the cans and are often willing to donate them free of charge for educational use.

- ...**Careful with your ceiling and light bulbs** – this experiment is really better done out-doors because the can does go up quite fast and high. It's also better outside because this experiment can get a little messy!

- ...**Using measuring syringes** - 10ml or 20ml syringes are really good for accurately measuring and putting the liquid into the cans. Most children find them easy enough to use, even the younger ones. If you do use them, simply draw the liquid from a small bowl or jug of water. And when using a syringe, please resist the temptation to use it as a squirt gun, particularly on other people! It may be great fun and even good science (there are all sorts of fun experiments you can do with syringes) but firing water – or something worse - at another person could actually cause some pain and be dangerous if caught in the eyes. And it should go without saying that you DO NOT use syringes with needles attached!

- ...**Broken tablets** – use several half-size pieces of tablet rather than whole ones when experimenting with different numbers of pieces, e.g., use one unbroken half, then break another half into two pieces, another half into several pieces and crush another half into many tiny pieces. You will find this a lot cheaper than breaking up whole tablets each time.

- ...**Don't eat the tablets** - some taste horrid and could make you very ill!

ANSWERS TO SOME OF THE NUMBERED QUESTIONS:

ANS. 3: The more tablet you use, the quicker the can will explode. Gas is produced where the water is in direct contact with the surface of the tablet. Larger amounts of tablet have more surface area than smaller amounts. The more surface area in touch with the water, the more gas is produced, the quicker the can explodes. Some people also report that the can goes higher with bigger pieces of tablet, though this is not always the case.

ANS. 4: The more fragments there are of a given size piece of tablet, the smaller they become, the quicker the can explodes. Smaller objects have bigger surface areas compared with their volumes than do larger objects. So if you broke a tablet into several pieces and measured their combined surface area, it would be much more than the surface area of the tablet before you broke it up. Remember from above that the more surface area in touch with the water, the more gas is produced, the quicker the can explodes.

ANS. 5: You'll find that the warmer the water, the quicker the can explodes. Remember from above that the tablet produces gas in water because of a chemical reaction. Most chemical reactions work more quickly in warmer temperatures. So the warmer the water, the more quickly gas is produced, the more quickly the can explodes.

ANS. 6: More acidic liquids, such as vinegar and lemon juice, make the can explode more quickly. This is because more acidic liquids cause the chemical reaction with the tablet to happen more quickly than do less acidic (or more alkali) liquids, such as water or milk.

ANS. 7: Other things you could try include: changing the amount of liquid, the type of tablet, the type of film can, the type of launch surface, which way up you place the can, and you could try fixing different size and weight coins or other objects to the outside of the can.

② LEVITATING BALLOONS & FLOATING BALLS

OBJECTIVE: To have fun exploring how to keep balloons, ping-pong balls and other objects floating in the air.

WHAT YOU NEED: Three or four rounded balloons, some different-shape balloons, one or two ping-pong or table-tennis balls, a thick bendy drinking straw (milk-shake type), and an electric blow hair-dryer (optional).

SOME OF THE SCIENCE YOU'RE EXPLORING: Chemistry, Physics & Biology: materials, gases, forces & motion, types of forces, pulling & pushing, gravity, friction & air-resistance, force & pressure, Ourselves: reflex response & breathing.

1 Bend a thick milk-shake straw into an 'L' shape.

2 Put the long end of the straw between your lips so that the shorter end is pointing straight up, then hold a balloon up just above the end of the straw and STAND VERY STILL.

3 While STANDING VERY STILL, blow into the straw and let go of the balloon, and keep on blowing steadily.

4 When you have had a go with one balloon, try a different size balloon.

© Dr Mark Biddiss 2001, 2005, 2011, Magical Science Book 1 @ www.Dr-Mark.co.uk

WHAT HAPPENS?

Provided that you keep the open end of the straw quite still and pointing upwards, the balloon will hover above the end of the straw for as long as you keep blowing steadily.

SOME QUESTIONS TO THINK ABOUT

1. What do you think is going on and in particular why do you think the balloon stays hovering without being blown away? (See 'SO WHAT'S GOING ON?')
2. Do you have to blow the same for any size balloon to keep them in the air at the same height, or do you have to blow harder for one size of balloon more than others? (answer provided)
3. Using the same balloon, what happens when you blow steadily harder than you did at first and then again not so hard?
4. Can you blow and keep the balloon hovering in the air without using a straw? (answer provided)
5. Can you make different shape balloons hover in the air, such as the long, sausage-shape ones? (answer provided)
6. Would you notice any difference in how hard you need to blow if you used a few balloons of the same shape and size but just of different colours? (answer provided)
7. Can you keep a table-tennis ball floating in the air instead of a balloon?
8. In this experiment, you used balloons and table tennis balls. Can you keep any small and lightweight objects hovering in the same way? (answer provided)
9. Would the diameter or thickness of the straw make any difference?
10. Why do people find it so difficult to **STAND VERY STILL** for this experiment? (answer provided)
11. What happens if you try all the experiments again but this time use an electric blow hair-dryer instead of a drinking straw? (see 'SO WHAT'S GOING ON?')

(numbered answers to most of the questions are given at the bottom of the next page)

SO WHAT'S GOING ON?

When you blow in one end of the drinking straw, you cause a stream or column of air to flow out and up into the air from the upward pointing end of the straw. The air moves fastest in the centre of the air-stream and more slowly further out. Fast moving air has less push or pressure than slower moving air. So each time the balloon drifts away from the centre of the air stream to one side, its quickly pushed back towards the middle again by the higher pressure of the slower moving air further out. The balloon hovers at a particular height because some of the air-stream blowing up from your drinking straw pushes up on the underside of the balloon before it flows up and around it.

You can also try these experiments using an electric blow hair-dryer instead of a milk-shake drinking straw and everything becomes so much easier! See how many table-tennis balls and balloons you can keep in the air at the same time; Dr Mark's record is two table-tennis balls and three different size balloons. Can you do better?

WHERE ON EARTH?

One of the things you should have discovered with this experiment was that the harder you blow, the higher the balloon or table-tennis ball hovers in the air. This phenomenon is used in some machines to measure the flow or amount of gas passing through them. One example would be the Boyles anaesthetic machine used in operating theatres in hospitals. The flow or amount of gas being used to keep the patient asleep under anaesthetic can be seen from reading the scale on a thin, transparent, vertical tube on the machine. Inside this tube is a little ball. As the anaesthetic gas flows up through this tube it pushes the little ball up with it. The more gas being used, the faster the flow, the higher the small ball hovers in the tube.

SOME TRICK TIPS!

- ...**Hyperventilation** - (or over-breathing) this is mainly caused by rapid shallow or deep breathing which leads to a high concentration of oxygen and not enough carbon dioxide in the blood stream. The most obvious symptoms to watch out for are numbness and tingling of the hands, feet and face, as well as the feeling of being dizzy, giddy or faint. To avoid hyperventilating, try to use deep, steady breaths when blowing and make sure you don't go for more than 4 or 5 minutes at a time on the activity without a minute or two break of breathing normally.

- ...**Asthma** - people with asthma or any other breathing difficulty need to be careful and may find this experiment more difficult to perform; but they should still have some fun!

- ...**Hygiene** - make sure everyone has their own drinking straw; people sharing each others spit is not a good idea!

- ...**Saliva Spray** - after a few minutes of blowing furiously through a drinking straw, deposits of saliva tend to build up in the straw. Try very hard to resist the temptation to spray spit in other peoples faces, or anywhere else for that matter!

- ...**Blow Balloon!** - if you find it difficult to keep the balloons in the air using a drinking straw, you can try blowing the balloons along a smooth floor instead, seeing how far you can blow different size balloons with a single big puff. It's a variation on Blow Football.

ANSWERS TO SOME OF THE NUMBERED QUESTIONS:

ANS.2: The smaller the balloon, the harder you'll need to blow to keep it hovering at a particular height. As I've said above, some of the air-stream blowing up from your drinking straw pushes up on the underside of the balloon before it flows up and around it. With bigger balloons, more of the up-blowing air-stream hits the balloon than when using smaller balloons. Or with smaller balloons, more of the air you blow flows up past the balloon without getting near enough to give it much of an upward push.

ANS.4: YES! You need to tip your head right back and look straight up. Then pucker-up your lips as if you wanted to kiss the balloon and blow steadily (you can kiss the balloon if you really want to).

ANS.5: YES! But you'll have to experiment with a few different shapes to see which are the easiest.

ANS.6: NO! Although, believe it or not, the colour could have an affect too small for you to notice. But how? (Clues: colour can affect the temperature both inside and immediately surrounding the balloon, and warmer air expands.)

ANS.8: NO! The general rule is that only roughly rounded, symmetrical, small and lightweight objects are likely to work. You could try a tightly screwed-up ball of paper or metal cooking foil.

ANS.10: For this experiment to work well you need to stand very still and keep the straw very still while blowing. Unless you make a conscious effort to achieve this there will be a natural reflex tendency to dance around beneath the balloon while trying to keep it hovering. You do this because every time you see the balloon drift to one side your natural reflex response is to move around to keep directly beneath it. It looks funny but it's not necessary!

© Dr Mark Biddiss 2001, 2005, 2011, Magical Science Book 1 @ www.Dr-Mark.co.uk

3. LOSING CONTROL

OBJECTIVE: To have fun exploring how we can stand without losing our balance and falling over.

WHAT YOU NEED: Yourself and perhaps a friend or two - you can easily do this experiment on yourself but it is more fun with a few friends!

SOME OF THE SCIENCE YOU'RE EXPLORING: Biology: ourselves, senses, vision, sense of balance.

1 Stand up straight with your arms folded in front of you. Then lift one of your feet a little off the floor and try to balance steadily on one leg.

2 When you are quite balanced, close your eyes tightly and keep them closed while you try to stay balanced.

© Dr Mark Biddiss 2001, 2005, 2011, Magical Science Book 1 @ www.Dr-Mark.co.uk

WHAT HAPPENS?

Within a few seconds of closing your eyes you should start to topple and lose your balance. You may fall over altogether!

SOME QUESTIONS TO THINK ABOUT

1. What do you think is going on? (see 'SO WHAT'S GOING ON?')

2. While you were balancing on one leg with your eyes **OPEN**, what could you feel happening with your foot and the calf-muscle in the back of your lower leg, between your knee and foot? (answer provided)

3. While you were balancing on one leg with your eyes **SHUT**, what could you feel happening with your foot and the calf-muscle in the back of your lower leg this time? (answer provided)

4. What happens if you repeat the experiment but this time stand with the other leg? (answer provided)

5. What happens if you repeat the experiment but this time close only one eye? (answer provided)

6. Do you think that a blind person would be able to balance on one leg better than a person with good eyesight? (answer provided)

(Numbered answers to most of the questions are given at the bottom of the next page)

SO WHAT'S GOING ON?

This trick illustrates how our brain and senses work together so that we can keep our balance. Three sets of sensors - located in our eyes (vision), muscles and joints, and inner ears - work together to help us detect position and motion in the various parts of our body so we can keep our balance. The sensors in our inner ear detect changes in motion and the orientation of our body. The sensors in our leg and arm muscles and joints detect the position and motion of our limbs. For most people, vision is an important sensory system in keeping balance because it provides visual information about our body's position with respect to the world around us. So, by closing your eyes, your brain no longer receives visual information, and thus it usually finds it more difficult to keep your body balanced.

WHERE ON EARTH?

Astronauts do a balance test similar to this one before and after they've been into space. They are normally asked to stand with both feet on the floor but with one foot directly behind and touching the other, toe-to-heel, as if they were walking along a tightrope or narrow beam.

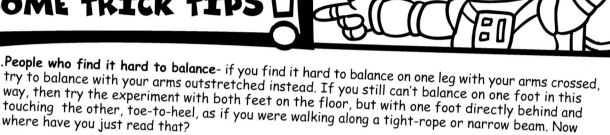

SOME TRICK TIPS!

...People who find it hard to balance- if you find it hard to balance on one leg with your arms crossed, try to balance with your arms outstretched instead. If you still can't balance on one foot in this way, then try the experiment with both feet on the floor, but with one foot directly behind and touching the other, toe-to-heel, as if you were walking along a tight-rope or narrow beam. Now where have you just read that?

ANSWERS TO SOME OF THE NUMBERED QUESTIONS:

ANS.2: You would have noticed your foot moving from side to side and your calf-muscle in the back of your lower leg twitching. Many of the position and motion sensors you need to keep balance are in your feet and legs. It's not easy to stay balanced on one leg and keep perfectly still. Remember that the sensors located in your eyes (vision), muscles and joints, and inner ears all send information to your brain to help you keep your balance. Each time you started to move out of balance, your brain knew this from the information it was receiving from its senses and a message was quickly sent to your muscles to move your body to get balanced again. So, for example, if you started tipping over to the right, your brain would get your muscles to move your body back over to the left. That's why you could feel your feet and leg muscles moving. You may have noticed in the past that when you lose your balance your reflex response is to throw your arms up and out; this helps slow down how quickly you topple. However, with your arms folded, the only muscles to move are in your feet and legs.

ANS.3: Almost straight after you closed your eyes, you should have noticed your foot and leg muscles start to move much more quickly than when you had your eyes open. This is because with your eyes shut, your brain cannot get accurate and fast enough information about how your body is moving. So with your eyes closed you tend to tip over more before your brain responds. Because you have tipped over more, your brain needs to move your muscles more to get you to tip back the other way. Your brain often over-compensates or moves your body too far the other way and the whole thing starts again. The net effect with your eyes closed is that your foot and leg muscles are working madly to keep you balanced. As you found out, it tends to get worse and worse!

ANS.4: There is a good chance that you will find it harder to keep your balance and you would probably topple more quickly. This is because many people find it easier to balance on one leg more than the other. The first time you did the experiment you probably stood on your best leg without even thinking about it.

ANS.5: Although you may not totally lose your balance, you'll probably still find it harder to balance than you did with both eyes open. You may also find it easier to balance with one particular eye open more than with the other eye. Remember that your brain expects information from both eyes to help you balance. If it only gets information from one eye, it doesn't get quite enough information and you'll likely find it harder to keep balance.

ANS.6: Probably YES! If the blind person has been blind for some time, their brain is used to not getting information from their eyes. So to balance, their brain tends to rely totally on the information it receives from the sets of sensors in their muscles and joints, and in their inner ears.

④ ORRIBLE OOZE

OBJECTIVE: To have fun exploring how some materials behave differently and change from one state into another, liquid to solid and solid to liquid albeit in a rather peculiar way!

WHAT YOU NEED: Cornflour (or cornstarch or custard powder), water, mixing bowl, small spoon and some 'orrid green food colouring!

SOME OF THE SCIENCE YOU'RE EXPLORING: Chemistry & Physics: properties of materials, liquids & solids, changing state, suspensions, mixtures, colloids, forces & motion, pressure, pushing & pulling.

1 Put three heaped teaspoons of cornflour into a mixing bowl and add a few drops of food colouring (optional).

2 Add water to the cornflour, only a spoonful at a time, while stirring and mixing the ooze with your fingers or the spoon. Keep adding water until you get a very thick, oozy, creamy mixture, which feels like a stiff liquid when you are stirring it VERY slowly.

3 See and feel what happens when you tap the surface of the ooze firmly with a finger or the spoon.

4 Pick up a handful of the ooze and squeeze it and roll it around firmly between your hands to make a ball. Then stop rolling and see what happens.

© Dr Mark Biddiss 2001, 2005, 2011, Magical Science Book 1 @ www.Dr-Mark.co.uk

WHAT HAPPENS?

Each time you tap the surface of your ooze very firmly with your finger or the spoon, the ooze feels like a fairly rigid solid, a bit like rubber; it may even crack (though apparently miraculously the crack almost immediately repairs itself again!). While you're rolling and squeezing your ooze between your hands, it feels like a slightly soft and pliable solid, very similar to modelling clay or plasticine. Almost immediately after you stop your rolling and squeezing, your ooze should flow out of your hand as a runny, messy, oozy slime! Wonderful stuff!

SOME QUESTIONS TO THINK ABOUT?

1. What do you think is going on? (see 'SO WHAT'S GOING ON?')
2. Try to repeat step 4 on the previous page. Can you roll the ooze back into a ball again? (answer provided)
3. How does it feel when you dip a finger in and out of the ooze and move the finger through the ooze - first moving your finger very slowly and then more quickly? (answer provided)
4. What happens when you rest small objects of different sizes and weights on the surface of the ooze.
5. If you should by chance find yourself standing knee-deep in ooze, what do you think would be the easiest way of getting out? (answer provided)
6. What do you think would be the quickest way of crossing a river of ooze without sinking in, assuming you didn't have your ooze-boat to hand? (answer provided)
7. Could you eat your ooze once you've finished playing , er I mean experimenting, with it? (answer provided)

(Numbered answers to most of the questions are given at the bottom of the next page)

SO WHAT'S GOING ON?

Scientists would call your ooze a non-Newtonian dilatant thixotropic fluid. The word 'dilatant' means 'stir thickening'. The word thixotropic comes from the Greek words thixis, which means the act of handling, and trope, which means change. When you mix cornflour (or cornstarch or custard powder) and water together it forms what's called a suspension or colloid: tiny, solid particles (of cornflour) suspended in a liquid (water).

Cornflour (or cornstarch) grains contain starch particles, or molecules, which are like long chains. While at rest your ooze is a thick liquid, just water with cornflour grains floating within it. However, when you add energy to the ooze by squeezing and rolling it around, three things occur: **1.** water is forced inside the grains of cornflour making them swell and get bigger; **2.** weak links are formed between the long starch molecular chains; and **3.** with so much less water outside and between the cornflour grains, they get squashed closer together and stick to each other. These three things result in the ooze becoming thicker and more viscous. The harder you apply force, the thicker, or more viscous, your ooze becomes. Most liquids don't actually behave quite like this at all!

WHERE ON EARTH?

Quicksand, a suspension of sand in water - is another thixotropic fluid that behaves very much like your ooze. So if you should by sad mischance fall into a pool of quicksand (or a pool of cornflour and water, for that matter), you now know what to do, don't you! Incidentally, it should be impossible for you to drown in deep quicksand (or ooze for that matter!) because your body should actually float much more easily than in water; just try to lay and slowly swim in the quicksand (or ooze) rather than try to stand up

Tomato Ketchup is yet another thixotropic fluid. From your experiments with your ooze, you might be able to figure out that the best way to get ketchup to flow out of the bottle and on to your food is to simply turn the bottle over and be patient and wait for it to come out! Vigorously shaking and smacking the bottom of the bottle actually slows the ketchup down! Why not try the same with your ooze to check?

SOME TRICK TIPS!

...**Add water a little at a time to get it right** - each time you add a little water, say, a small spoonful (about 5ml), mix it completely into your developing ooze before you add any more. If you mix in some water and your ooze appears to be like a crumbly, flaky solid, it means that you need to add a little more water. If your ooze gets very runny like a thick liquid, it means that you've added too much water. In this case you simply need to add a little more cornflour.

...**Stirring and mixing** - you'll probably find that as soon as you've added only your first few drops of water to the cornflour, it will become impossible to stir your mixture like you would a cup of tea or coffee. The best ways to mix your ooze now is either use your fingers or repeatedly stab and twist your small spoon down into the mix.

...**Add colour at the right time** - if you do want coloured ooze (green looks great), you need to add a few drops of your food colouring BEFORE you start adding and mixing in your water. If you add the liquid food colouring AFTER you've added your water and got your mix just right, your ooze will then turn runny because you've effectively added too much water.

Don't wash your ooze down the sink or toilet, it might cause a blockage in the pipes! If you let it dry out you can re-use the powder again!

ANSWERS TO SOME OF THE NUMBERED QUESTIONS:

ANS.2: YES! Amazingly, if you gather the runny, oozy mess back between your hands and start squeezing and rolling again, it turns back into a solid ball! Weird or what?

ANS.3: The faster you try to move your finger in and out and through the ooze, the more force you need to apply, or the harder your ooze tries to stop you! Also, when you try quickly to lift and remove your finger right out of the ooze, some clings hard to your finger as if trying to pull you back down. If you lift your finger much more slowly, hardly any ooze clings to your finger and you can pull it out very easily! Spooky aye?

ANS.5: From your experiments you should be able to figure out that the easiest way to get your legs free would be to lift each leg out of the ooze nice and slowly.

ANS.6: The quickest way would be to run hard and fast across the river. The longer you keep your feet on one spot, the more your feet will sink into the ooze. Stomping your feet firmly down as you run will also help to keep you out of the ooze. You could probably run on the spot like this without sinking in either!

ANS.7: YES! (Though I can't imagine why you'd want to, oh YUK!) You can eat your ooze if you really want to provided that you've used clean water, bowl, spoon, hands, and anything else that's been in contact with your ooze. (I have to admit that I've eaten some ooze myself out of curiosity - to me it had a powdery texture and little or no taste; it also got stuck to my teeth and gums, so I recommend a cup of water to rinse your mouth and wash it down!)

© Dr Mark Biddiss 2001, 2005, 2011, Magical Science Book 1 @ www.Dr-Mark.co.uk

⑤ SCREAMING STRAWS & RASPBERRY BALLOONS

OBJECTIVE: To have fun exploring how to make a drinking straw scream and screech in different ways, and how to get balloons make a raspberry or farting sound.

WARNING: REALLY IRRITATING EXPERIMENT!

WHAT YOU NEED: A thick drinking straw (milk-shake type), a long balloon and a pair of scissors.

SOME OF THE SCIENCE YOU'RE EXPLORING: Physics: Physical Processes: forces & motion, transfer of energy, sound, air, force & pressure, friction, air-resistance, amplitude, pitch, frequency.

1 Flatten one end of a thick drinking straw using your fingers or by sliding it between your front teeth.

2 With some scissors, carefully cut the flattened end of the straw into a slightly blunted point. This makes two pointed, triangular flaps.

Snip here

3 Squeeze the flattened, cut end of the straw between your lips and blow hard.

TIP! If you do not get a sound straight away, try changing how hard you squeeze the straw between your lips and how hard you blow. You may need to change both squeezing and blowing to get a steady sound. It is not always easy so be patient!

© Dr Mark Biddiss 2001, 2005, 2011, Magical Science Book 1 @ www.Dr-Mark.co.uk

WHAT HAPPENS?

If you blow and squeeze the straw between your lips just right, you'll hear a loud, high-pitched 'duck call' or screaming sound! It's the perfect family alarm call for 6 a.m. on Sunday morning!

SOME QUESTIONS TO THINK ABOUT

1. What do you think is going on? (see **'SO WHAT'S GOING ON?'**)
2. Is the screaming sound the same if you use wider or narrower straws of the same length? (answer provided)
3. What happens to the sound you make if you cut the straw to shorter lengths? (answer provided)
4. What happens to the sound you make if you cut a small hole anywhere along the length of the straw? (answer provided)
5. What happens to the sound you make if you cut two or more small holes along the length of the straw, and use your fingers to cover different holes as you blow?
6. If you fitted a paper sleeve to the end of your straw (or slide on a straw with a slightly different diameter) and change the overall length of your straw and sleeve by sliding the sleeve backwards and forwards while you blow, what happens to the sound you make? (answer provided)
7. Can you make the screaming sound if you turn the straw around and this time put the other uncut and unflattened end in your mouth, with the two flaps now pointing way from you? (answer provided)
8. Take a long balloon and cut off the closed end so that you've made a flattened rubber tube, open at both ends. Now cut the pointed flaps onto that cut end of the balloon, the same as you did with your straw in box 2 on the previous page. What sort of sound do you make if you put the uncut end of the balloon into your mouth and blow as if you were trying to inflate the balloon? (answer provided)

(Numbered answers to most of the questions are given at the bottom of the next page)

SO WHAT'S GOING ON?

When you blow air in between the two triangular-shaped plastic flaps or 'reeds', the pressure of the air between the flaps goes down. This causes a suction effect which makes the flaps close together. When that happens, no more air flows and so the slightly elastic flaps open up again. Then more air blows in between, which causes the flaps to close again, and the same thing happens. This keeps happening very fast and that's why the flaps open and close very fast. This is the 'tingly vibration' you can feel on your lips.

Every time the reeds open and close, it sends a tiny puff, or wave of air along the straw tube and out the open end. With the reeds opening and closing so fast, this sends lots of tiny puffs or waves of air down the tube. This causes the air in the tube to resonate or vibrate, and you hear this as a 'screaming' sound wave coming from the straw.

© Dr Mark Biddiss 2001, 2005, 2011, Magical Science Book 1 @ www.Dr-Mark.co.uk

WHERE ON EARTH?

Some musical wind instruments, such as the clarinet, use vibrating reeds to make the sound in the same way as the reeds on your screaming straw. Similarly, you can control the note you hear from some of these instruments by changing the length of the tube through which the sound wave is travelling, such as with the oboe. Wind-powered organs like the ones you often find in churches use a different tube for each note. So they will have many tubes, each one being a different length to the others.

SOME TRICK TIPS!

- **Practice & Patience** - Creating the screaming sound with the drinking straw is not the easiest activity, particularly for younger children, and it may take a few minutes of trial and error to get it right; but keep at it and you will succeed! (5 year-olds have been able to do this experiment within 5 minutes)

- **Hyperventilation** - (or over-breathing) this is mainly caused by rapid shallow or deep breathing which leads to a high concentration of oxygen and not enough carbon dioxide in the blood stream. The most obvious symptoms to watch out for are numbness and tingling of the hands, feet and face, as well as the feeling of being dizzy, giddy or faint. To avoid hyperventilating, try to use deep, steady breaths when blowing and make sure you don't go for more than 4 or 5 minutes at a time on the activity without a minute or two break of breathing normally.

- **Asthma** - people with asthma or any other breathing difficulty need to be careful and may find the experiment with the straw more difficult to perform; but they should still have some fun!

- **Hygiene** - make sure everyone has their own drinking straw and balloon; people sharing each other's spit is not a good idea!

- **Saliva Spray** - after a few minutes of blowing furiously, deposits of saliva tend to build up in the straw and balloon. Try very hard to resist the temptation to spray spit in other people's faces, or anywhere else for that matter!

ANSWERS TO SOME OF THE NUMBERED QUESTIONS:

Ans.2: NO! Wider straws produce louder screams. The width or diameter of the straw controls the loudness or amplitude of the sound wave produced. A wider straw allows taller or wider sound waves - or waves with a bigger amplitude. The bigger the amplitude of the sound wave, the louder the sound will be.

Ans.3: The squeakiness or pitch (or frequency) of the sound note you hear depends upon the length of the straw. This is because the length of the straw affects the length of the sound waves produced by the vibrating flaps or reeds. Longer straws produce longer sound waves, which have a lower frequency and thus deeper or lower pitch. Therefore, shorter straws produce shorter sound waves, which have higher pitch.

Ans.4: I said above that the squeakiness or pitch of the note you hear depends upon the length of the straw. Cutting a hole anywhere along the length of the straw produces a higher pitch note. This is because by cutting the hole, you are effectively shortening the length of the tube along which the sound wave is produced; remember from above that the shorter the tube, the higher the pitch of the sound produced. An interesting point to note is that the pitch of the sound you make with a cut hole is about the same as that produced if you were to completely cut and shorten the straw at the same position of the cut hole, as long as the hole is big enough.

Ans.6: Sliding the sleeve backwards and forwards changes the overall length of the tube and thus the note you hear. You will have made a straw oboe! Remember from above that the note or pitch you hear depends on the length of the tube.

Ans.7: YES! You can make the sound but you'll need to suck hard instead of blowing hard. Think about why.

Ans.8: You should make a wonderful flatulent raspberry or farting sound! The great thing about this experiment is that you can see the flaps as they flap back and forth, or vibrate. An interesting thing to consider is what 'flaps back and forth' in our bodies when we make that sound? (And remember that we can make that sound from two different places in our bodies, so you'll need to think about what is 'flapping' in each case!)

6. PHANTOM PENCILS

OBJECTIVE: To have fun exploring the sense of touch and how easily it can be fooled.

WHAT YOU NEED: Two or more sharpened pencils (though not too sharp!) and a friend. You can do this experiment on yourself but it is not so effective and it's much more fun with a friend anyway!

SOME OF THE SCIENCE YOU'RE EXPLORING: Biology: ourselves, senses, skin, illusions.

1. Hold two sharpened pencils side-by-side. Make sure their pointed ends are lined up.

2. Ask a friend to hold out one of their arms with the palm of their hand facing upwards. Ask them to roll up any sleeve to their elbow and to close their eyes tightly. Tell them to keep VERY STILL.

3. GENTLY press the two pencil points against one of your friend's finger-tips and ask them how many points they can feel. Try this again on two or three of their other fingertips.

4. Now do the same thing on several different places on their bare arms.

TIP: Your friend will find it easier to keep their arm still if you get them to rest it against a steady surface, such as on a tabletop.

© Dr Mark Biddiss 2001, 2005, 2011, Magical Science Book 1 @ www.Dr-Mark.co.uk

WHAT HAPPENS?

When you press the two points together on your friend's fingertips, they should feel two separate points quite easily. However, when you do the same thing on their arm, they'll probably mostly only feel one point touching them. It's as if one of the pencils is not really there and has become a phantom - spooky!

SOME QUESTIONS TO THINK ABOUT

1. What do you think is going on? (see 'SO WHAT'S GOING ON?')

2. How many points can your friend feel on their arm if you hold the two pencils with a bigger gap between the points? (You can do this by holding the pencils in the shape of an "X") (answer provided)

3. Why is it more effective to ask the person being prodded to close their eyes? (answer provided)

4. What are the results if you try the same experiment using three or more pencils?

5. Ask your friend if you can try the same experiment on one of their legs somewhere below their knee. What are the results this time?

6. Why do you think we have some areas of skin, such as on our fingertips, with so many more touch receptors than other areas, making them more sensitive, with greater acuity? (answer provided)

7. What are the results if you try the same experiments using less sharply pointed pencil tips or even more sharply pointed tips or a mixture of both? (**Be careful with the sharper points!**)

(Numbered answers and explanations to some of the questions are given on the next page)

SO WHAT'S GOING ON?

We can feel things touching us because we have about half a million tiny (microscopic) touch sensors, or touch receptors, all over our body buried just under the dead surface layer of our skin. A touch receptor is activated by a touch 'stimulus', such as a pencil point touching our skin. Some areas of the skin, such as the lips and fingertips, are much more sensitive to touch than other areas, such as the back of the legs and arms. The more touch sensitive areas of skin have many more touch receptors clustered together in the same area than do less sensitive areas of skin. Our sense of touch can be extremely fine. In areas of high touch sensitivity, such as our fingertips, we can tell when there are two points touching us even when only a very tiny distance separates them. This sense ability is called 'acuity' - how close two points can be before the sensation they cause blends to feel like one point. And as you have discovered, your acuity is quite different at different places on your body. Even the smallest, lightest touch, or stimulus, in the more sensitive areas of our skin is likely to trigger at least a few touch receptors. That same touch may not even be felt on less sensitive areas where there are far fewer receptors.

WHERE ON EARTH?

Your skin isn't the only part of your body that has more sensitive areas than others. The surface of your eye is like this too. The white part of your eye feels hardly anything compared with the coloured part. In fact, you can VERY GENTLY touch and push the white part of your eye without causing any pain at all. Definitely DON'T do that with the coloured part though!

SOME TRICK TIPS!

- **...YOU MUST NOT STAB EACH OTHER!** - to avoid this, especially with sharper pencils, don't press too hard on your friend's skin. You only need to press GENTLY!

- **...Tell your friend to keep very still** - if they move around while you press the pencil points against their skin they are more likely to be able to tell how many points there are touching them. A better way of doing this experiment is to get your friend to rest their arm (or leg) against a steady surface.

- **...Use a Compass or Dividers** - instead of using two pencils you could use a geometry compass (for drawing circles) or a pair of dividers. This would more easily allow you to very accurately alter and measure the distance between the two points. You will also be able to bring the points much more closely together using one of these geometry instruments. But be especially careful with the sharp points often found on these instruments! If you're worried about using the sharp points you could fix your two pencils to the 'arms' of the compass or dividers instead.

ANSWERS TO SOME OF THE NUMBERED QUESTIONS:

ANS.2: When you hold your pencils side-by-side the points are usually between about 6 to 8mm apart with 'normal' width pencils. You'll probably find that you have to increase the distance between the points to more than 40 or 50mm - 4 or 5cm - before your friend feels the two points separately. Since your friend's arm has far fewer touch receptors in the skin than in the skin of their fingertips, it's less likely that both pencil points will each stimulate a receptor when the points are too close together.

ANS.3: If your friend watches what you are doing they will see when you are using two closely spaced points on their arm. And even if they can't actually 'feel' two points touching their skin, they are more likely to 'sense' two because they can 'see' two. Their brain will combine the sensory information it is getting from their eyes and their skin to conclude that there are two points touching them. Asking them to close their eyes means that their brain only has the sensory information from the skin to work on.

ANS.6: Some areas of our skin are more sensitive than others because we need them to be so. For example, we use our fingertips all the time in many different touch activities. We need them to be sensitive enough to feel small details and differences in touch. We don't usually use the back of our arms or lower legs in the same way and so they don't need to be so sensitive to touch.

© Dr Mark Biddiss 2001, 2005, 2011, Magical Science Book 1 @ www.Dr-Mark.co.uk

⑦ BLACK MAGIC & SECRET COLOURS

★ OBJECTIVE:
To have fun exploring the secret colours hidden in black and other coloured inks, and in food colouring.

SOME OF THE SCIENCE YOU'RE EXPLORING:
Chemistry: separating colours using chromatography, capillary action, solvents, solutes, pigments.

WHAT YOU NEED:
A black felt-tip marker pen (non-permanent or water-based ink and NOT permanent ink), a few other different coloured marker pens (green, brown and purple are good), dry white blotting-paper (or coffee filter paper), water, a clothes washing-line peg (or paperclip), a cup (preferably see-through), food dye or colouring (green and black are good).

1 Pour some water in a cup, about 1cm deep.

2 Cut a dry piece of white blotting-paper (or coffee filter paper) into a strip about 2- or 3cm wide and long enough to hang down the inside of the cup, from the top edge to the bottom.

3 With a black felt-tip marker pen, draw a small black round spot, about 3 or 4mm in size and about 2cm from one end of the paper strip. Instead of a round dot you could draw a thick line (about 2mm wide) across the width of the strip and about 2cm from one end.

4 Carefully lower the blotting-paper strip down the inside of the cup until it trails into the water. Fix the strip in place with the peg or paper-clip to the top rim of the cup, making sure that the black spot or line is just a few millimetres ABOVE the surface level of the water. Now watch for five to ten minutes.

WHAT HAPPENS?

Within a few minutes, you'll see the water soaking in and flowing upwards through the blotting-paper strip. As the water passes up through the black ink mark, you'll start to see some different colours working their way up towards the top of the strip with the water. If all goes well, you should see the colours that were used to mix the black ink separate out as they flow up the paper strip. Some colours will separate out higher up on the paper strip than others.

SOME QUESTIONS TO THINK ABOUT

1. What do you think is going on? (see 'SO WHAT'S GOING ON?')

2. After about ten minutes, how many different colours can you see going up the strip?

3. What colours do you see when you use different colour pens, such as brown, purple or green?

4. What other things (variables) could you change to explore what happens? (some suggestions provided)

5. Using the same experiment idea you started with, how could you discover what coloured pigments have been used to make the different colours on sugar-coated sweets or candy, or different coloured food dyes, or paints? (purple, brown, black and green colourings work well) (answer provided)

6. Using the experiment idea you tried in question 5, what would be the result if you tested for the pigments used in a mix of several different colour sugar-coated candy sweets tested together at the same time, or a mix a few different coloured food dyes tested together?

(Numbered answers and explanations to some of the questions are given on the next page)

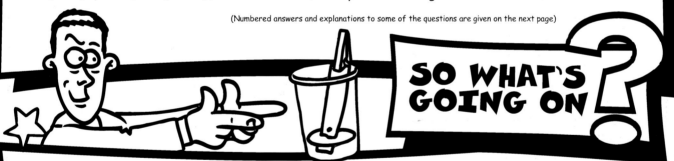

SO WHAT'S GOING ON?

In this experiment the colours are formed by a process called Chromatography (the name comes from the Greek words chroma which means colour, and graph which means writing). Many coloured inks, dyes and other pigments are made by mixing different colours together. For example, black ink is not usually made from a black pigment but from a combination of other coloured pigments such as cyan, magenta and yellow. Most non-permanent coloured inks are made with pigments that dissolve in water. When we draw on a piece of paper with ink, the water in the ink eventually evaporates and dries out, leaving the dry pigment(s) on the paper. In our experiments above, the water from the bottom of the cup travels up through the blotting-paper (by a process called capillary action) and passes through the black ink mark we made with the felt-pen. As it travels up through the black mark, the water (the solvent) dissolves the pigments (the solutes) in the ink and carries them along with it. Different coloured pigments are carried along at different rates; some travel farther and faster than others. How far and how fast a particular coloured pigment travels through the blotting-paper depends on the size of the pigment particles, or molecules, and on how strongly the pigment, water and paper molecules are attracted to each other (remember that atoms and molecules are the building blocks of practically every substance in the Universe). Since the water carries the different pigments at different rates, the black ink separates to reveal the different coloured pigments that were mixed to make it.

© Dr Mark Biddiss 2001, 2005, 2011, Magical Science Book 1 @ www.Dr-Mark.co.uk

WHERE ON EARTH?

Chromatography is one of the most valuable techniques scientists can use for separating out mixtures of different substances or chemicals. It was first developed early in the twentieth century by a Russian botanist called Mikhail Tsvet. He used it to explore the different pigments that made up different plant dyes. There are different types of chromatography; some use liquid (called liquid chromatography) as you did in your experiment, and some use gas (called gas chromatography). Chromatography is especially useful for detecting the tiniest amounts or traces of a substance within a mixture. Scientists use chromatography to find out about such things as:

.....the chemical ingredients that make up a mixture of gases, such as the air we breath;

.....the chemical ingredients in mixtures that give us particular scents, tastes and flavours;

.....the different substances found in blood and urine (such as drugs and the products of illness and disease);

.....the polluting chemical substances in the atmosphere and in the water of our rivers, lakes and oceans.

SOME TRICK TIPS!

...Different liquid solvent for different pigments- in this experiment I suggested using non-permanent or water-based pigments, inks and dyes (your solutes), so that you could use water as your solvent. Water won't be much good for permanent or non-water soluble solutes because they don't normally dissolve in water. However if you do want to explore what happens with permanent or non-water based pigments, you could try a different solvent such as acetone (nail varnish remover), methylated spirits or alcohol. Just remember to check any safety instructions about the solvents you try, since some can be dangerous if not used and handled properly.

ANSWERS TO SOME OF THE NUMBERED QUESTIONS:

ANS. 4: Other things you could change and explore include:

- .....the type of liquid solvent used (for example, instead of water you could try cooking oil, acetone or nail-varnish remover, alcohol, methylated spirits, dilute washing up liquid, etc.). Remember to read any safety instructions about the solvents you try;
- .....different temperature solvent;
- .....different paper (such as different brands of coffee filter-paper, blotting paper or paper towels);
- .....different makes or brands of pigment (such as two or three different brands of black ink pens, black food dyes or black paints; not forgetting other colours, of course);
- .....other coloured substances (such as coffee, paint and tea);
- .....the distance different colour pigments (and different brands of the same colour pigment) travel along the paper;
- .....the time taken for different pigments (of different brands and solvent temperatures) to travel along the paper;

ANS. 5: One way of exploring for the colours used in coloured sugar-coated candy sweets is to put several candy sweets of the same colour into the water in the cup. Purple, brown or green candy sweets are good to try first. You only really need just enough water to wet the candy sweets and to be able to stir them around to help dissolve and wash off the coloured pigments in their coating into the water (slightly warm water will work better than cold water). Since the pigments are now dissolved in the water, you don't need to draw anything on your blotting or coffee filter paper. Just carry on with your investigation as described in step 4 of what to do. I call this experiment Candy Chromatography! When investigating liquid pigments, such as food dye or paint, either use these instead of water, or mix some into the water and, again, carry on from step 4.

⑧ DIVING PEN-TOPS & ORANGE-PEEL

OBJECTIVE:
To have fun exploring how to make objects float and sink in a bottle without touching the objects and to look at the idea behind submarines.

SOME OF THE SCIENCE YOU'RE EXPLORING:
Chemistry & Physics: Properties of materials: liquids & gases, density, floating & sinking, physical changes; Physical processes: forces & motion, gravity, force & pressure, unbalanced forces.

WHAT YOU NEED:
A plastic (preferably see-through) pen-top with pocket-clip, an empty see-through plastic bottle with the screw-on cap, some modelling clay, a tall drinking-glass or measuring jug or bowl, some fresh orange peel and some water.

1 If your pen-top has a small air-hole at the narrow end, you will need to completely block this off with a small piece of modelling clay or putty. Blocking it off with a small ball of putty from the inside works well (push the putty up inside). Then fix some modelling putty around the pocket-clip of the pen-top, making sure NOT to completely block up the entrance hole where the pen would slide in.

Block hole if needed

2 Initially, you need to fix enough modelling clay to weight the pen-top so that it only just floats (pocket-clip and wide open end downwards) and is just on the point of sinking. Try it in a tall drinking glass, measuring jug or bowl full of water until you get it just right.

3 Completely fill your plastic bottle with water, carefully lower your correctly weighted pen-top into the plastic bottle and carefully screw the bottle cap on tightly.

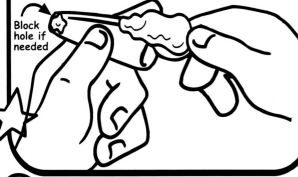

4 Squeeze the plastic bottle quite hard with both hands, hold for a few seconds and then release your squeeze.

© Dr Mark Biddiss 2001, 2005, 2011, Magical Science Book 1 @ www.Dr-Mark.co.uk

WHAT HAPPENS?

When you squeeze the bottle, the pen-top diver sinks. When you stop squeezing, it floats up to the top again!

SOME QUESTIONS TO THINK ABOUT

1. What do you think is going on? (see 'SO WHAT'S GOING ON?')
2. Can you make the pen-top diver sink more quickly or more slowly? (answer provided)
3. Can you make the diver float in the same place, without it moving much up or down, in different parts of the bottle (such as about half-way down)? (answer partly provided)
4. In step 1 on the last page you were told NOT to completely block up the entrance hole of the pen-lid with putty (the hole next to the pocket-clip where the pen would slide in). What results do you get, and why, if you DO completely block it with putty? (answer provided)
5. Do you think you could use a glass bottle instead of a plastic bottle in this experiment? (answer provided)
6. What other things (variables) could you change to explore what happens? (some suggestions provided)

(Numbered answers and explanations to some of the questions are given on the next page)

SO WHAT'S GOING ON?

You have made a version of what is known as Descartes Diver, or more often called a Cartesian Diver, which was originally invented in the seventeenth century! The plastic pen-top and modelling putty are both denser and thus heavier than the water (they displace) and so would usually sink. However, in the way you have made and placed your diver (pen-top and putty) into the water, a bubble of air is trapped inside the pen-top and this is just big enough to make the whole diver float. It floats because the diver as a whole (pen-top, putty, air bubble and a little water inside) is actually now less dense than the same volume of water it takes up (or displaces).

When you squeeze the plastic bottle, you also squeeze the water inside. Now it's very difficult to squeeze water (or any liquid) to make it take up less space. So when you squeeze the bottle, you squeeze the water and push it into any air spaces that may be left in the bottle. Because you completely filled the bottle with water, the only place the water can go is up into the diver itself. The water squeezes the air-bubble inside the diver and makes it smaller (because gases, and remember that air is a mix of several gases - are quite easy to squeeze into a smaller space). The smaller air-bubble is now not big and buoyant enough to keep the whole diver floating and so the diver as a whole becomes denser and heavier than the water it displaces, and sinks. When you stop squeezing the bottle, you also stop squeezing the water up into the pen-top and this allows the pressure in the squeezed bubble to push the water back out and expand again until it is big enough to float the diver up.

You can also use small pieces of orange peel as your divers instead of the pen-top and putty. These work because the whitish, pithy part of orange peel contains tiny bubbles of air, which make them float. Though you'll probably have to squeeze pretty hard to sink the orange peel!

WHERE ON EARTH?

The scientific principle behind your pen-top Cartesian Diver is used to make submarines sink and float. A submarine has large tanks called ballast tanks built into it. When the sub needs to sink deeper, seawater from outside the sub is pumped into the ballast tanks. This increases the overall density of the sub, making it heavier than the water it displaces and so the sub sinks. When the sub needs to come up or to float on the surface of the water, compressed air is pumped from compressed air tanks into the ballast tanks. The air forces the seawater out of the tanks and the sub, which decreases the overall density of the sub, making it lighter than the water it displaces and so it floats up. So, the sub sinks or floats according to how much air and water is in the ballast tanks. To stay floating at the same depth underwater, the sub needs to have just the right amount of air and water in the ballast tanks so that the overall density of the sub is the same as that of the surrounding seawater it displaces at that particular depth.

SOME TRICK TIPS!

- ...**Try to get a see-through or transparent pen-top-** then you'll be able to see what happens to the size of the bubble when you squeeze and release the bottle.

- ...**Don't drop the bottle-** if you do, some of the air may escape from your diver causing it to sink permanently. Then you'll have to get the diver out of the bottle, tip the water out of the diver and put it back in again.

ANSWERS TO SOME OF THE NUMBERED QUESTIONS:

ANS. 2: YES! Squeeze hard and it sinks faster, squeeze more gently and it sinks more slowly. The harder you squeeze the bottle, the harder the water squeezes the air bubble inside the diver, which in turn makes the bubble even smaller and so less buoyant.

ANS. 3: YES! (But it takes a bit of practice and a steady hand!) Though I'll leave it to you to figure out just how (clue: see 'WHERE ON EARTH?' above).

ANS. 4: If you completely block the wide entrance opening of your diver with putty you will be able to get it to float OK but you won't be able to get it to sink, however hard you squeeze. This is because the water outside can't get in to squeeze the bubble inside.

ANS. 5: NO & YES! The answers NO if you use a glass bottle with a screw-on cap, because you can't squeeze a hard and rigid glass bottle to make it squeeze the water inside. The answers YES, but to be able to make the diver dive, you'll have to fit a piece of fairly tough and stretchy rubber (say, from a balloon) over the mouth of the bottle INSTEAD of a screw-on lid. To make the diver sink you push firmly down onto the rubber with your thumb, as if you were trying to push your thumb through the rubber into the top of the bottle.

ANS. 6: Other things you could change and explore include:

.....Using different size plastic bottles;

.....What happens if you try the experiment but without completely filling the bottle with water (say, a quarter-full, half-full, three-quarters full and almost full)?

.....Trying thicker liquids instead of water, such as cooking oil and treacle;

.....Put in two or more divers at the same time;

.....Try to think of ways of making your diver with different materials instead of pen-tops and putty; why not try using eyedroppers or plastic pipettes, for instance?

© Dr Mark Biddiss 2001, 2005, 2011, Magical Science Book 1 @ www.Dr-Mark.co.uk

⑨ HOLEY HANDS

OBJECTIVE: To have fun exploring how to see through a hole in your hand, as well as through other objects.

WHAT YOU NEED: A cardboard or plastic tube about 20 to 25cm long and 3 or 4cm wide, or a sheet of paper rolled up to make a tube.

SOME OF THE SCIENCE YOU'RE EXPLORING: Living Things: Ourselves: senses, vision & seeing.

1 With your right hand, hold the tube up to your right eye and look straight ahead through it as if it was a telescope. At the same time, cover your left eye with your left hand, with the palm of your hand facing and very close to your left eye and the edge of your left hand just touching the side of the tube.

2 Keeping both eyes open, slowly move your left hand forward and away from your left eye, sliding your hand out along the tube.

WOW!

© Dr Mark Biddiss 2001, 2005, 2011, Magical Science Book 1 @ www.Dr-Mark.co.uk

WHAT HAPPENS?

At some point it should look as if you are peering through a hole in your left hand!

SOME QUESTIONS TO THINK ABOUT?

1. What do you think is going on? (see 'SO WHAT'S GOING ON?')
2. What appears to happen to the size of the hole in your hand as you move your hand further away from your face? (answer provided)
3. What appears to happen to the hole in your hand if you tilt and sweep the tube around to the left and right and up and down, without moving your head or your left hand?
4. What happens to the hole in your hand if you close your right eye (that is the eye you are using to look through the tube)?
5. Try the same experiment but this time look through the tube with your left eye and at your right hand with your right eye. Do you still get the same effect?
6. Try the same experiment using something else instead of your left hand; perhaps you could see a hole in your arm, foot (could be tricky), leg, a book or somebody elses hand!

(The answer and explanation to question 2 is given on the next page)

SO WHAT'S GOING ON?

Obviously, your brain is getting very confused! Your brain is used to getting pretty similar images from each eye, which it can easily combine to make a single clear and sensible image. In this experiment your right eye sees the image coming through the tube and your left eye sees your open hand. Your brain justcan't sort them out sensibly and instead simply combines the two images together, trying to make as much sense as possible. The result is that you see the illusion of a hole in your hand! Not very sensible really!

WHERE ON EARTH?

An important reason for us having two eyes is that your brain actually wants to get two slightly different (though very similar) images, one from each eye. The two images are different because your eyes have a short distance between them and so are not in the same place at the same time. Your brain needs these two slightly different images so that it can better judge how far different objects are away from us and from each other, particularly objects very close to us. You can see this effect very clearly with another simple experiment: hold an upwards-pointing finger in front of your face and look beyond it at something farther away in the distance, such as the other side of the room (the further away the better). Notice what things in the distance appear to line up with your upwards-pointing finger. Now close your right eye while looking at the same scene with your left eye. Notice if your finger still appears to line up with the same objects further away in the distance. If it does, open your right eye and this time close your left eye. Now what do you see? With only one eye open you will notice that your finger appears to line up with distant objects differently to when you have both eyes open. For some people that happens only with one particular eye shut, with others, with either eye shut.

SOME TRICK TIPS!

...Try looking through the tube at things near and in the distance- some people find it easier to see this illusion well by looking through the tube at something far away. Others may find it easier to see the illusion when looking at much nearer things.

ANSWERS TO SOME OF THE NUMBERED QUESTIONS:

ANS. 2: For most people, the hole in your hand appears to get bigger as you move your hand further away from your eye. This is actually an extra illusion (WOW! Two illusions at the same time!). If you concentrate really hard and watch very closely, you'll notice that the hole doesn't actually get any bigger at all; it stays exactly the same size. What happens is that your hand appears to get smaller as you move it further away from your eye, as you'd probably expect. And because your brain is having enough trouble as it is trying to combine the two very different images from each eye, it takes a best guess and combines the two images together to appear as if the hole is getting bigger as you move your hand away! Not a particularly good guess, but it's the best it can do with the information it has.

10. BAG BOMBS & BLOWING-UP BALLOONS

OBJECTIVE: To have fun exploring how to explode plastic bags and create self-inflating balloons.

WARNING: VERY SMELLY EXPERIMENT!

WHAT YOU NEED: Baking soda (or bicarbonate of soda or bicarb), vinegar, water (preferably warm), paper towel or tissue, see-through zip-lock plastic bag (they're the ones you can seal up and make air-tight), large spoon, measuring jug or cup, balloon, small funnel and a small bottle with a narrow neck (to fit balloon on).

SOME OF THE SCIENCE YOU'RE EXPLORING: Chemistry & Physics: Properties of materials: solids, liquids and gases, dissolving, chemical reactions, rates of reaction, acids & bases, Physical processes: forces & motion, pressure, power & energy.

1 Test your zip-lock bag for leaks by filling it with water, close it up, tip it upside-down and give it a gentle squeeze. If no water leaks out, it should work just fine. If it leaks, try another one.

2 Pour into your plastic bag about a quarter of a cup (about 50ml) of water (preferably warm) and about half a cup (about 100ml) of vinegar.

Wrap about 1½ tablespoons of baking soda in a square of paper towel or tissue.

3 Zip-close your bag about halfway, carefully put your baking soda packet into the bag and then fully zip-close the bag as quickly as possible.

4 Give the bag a good shake, quickly put it in the sink, bath or on the ground outside and stand well back!

© Dr Mark Biddiss 2001, 2005, 2011, Magical Science Book 1 @ www.Dr-Mark.co.uk

WHAT HAPPENS?

Within a few seconds you will see bubbles forming in the bag and the bag begins to swell and get bigger. Very soon the bag should explode with a bang! Most of the vinegar and water mix will have turned to foam.

SOME QUESTIONS TO THINK ABOUT

1. What do you think is going on?   (see 'SO WHAT'S GOING ON?')
2. Why did I tell you to wrap the baking soda in a piece of paper towel or tissue? (answer provided)
3. What happens if you wrap the baking soda more loosely (make a tissue envelope) or more tightly?
4. What happens if you wrap the baking soda in more layers of paper towel or tissue?
5. What happens if you use more or less baking soda?
6. What happens if you use more or less vinegar?
7. What happens if you use more or less water?
8. What other things (variables) could you change to explore what happens? (some suggestions provided)
9. Using the above ideas, how could you cause a balloon to apparently inflate itself (clue: you might use the small funnel and bottle)? (suggestion provided)

(Numbered answers and explanations to some of the questions are given on the next page)

SO WHAT'S GOING ON?

When you mix baking soda (or bicarbonate of soda) with vinegar a chemical reaction takes place and carbon dioxide gas is produced. Vinegar is an acid and the baking soda is a base and the carbon dioxide gas is produced as a result of this acid-base reaction. The carbon dioxide gas helps produce (along with the vinegar and water) the bubbling foam you see inside the bag (foam is made up of thousands of tiny bubbles). This causes the bag to inflate and explode. Adding water means that you don't have to use so much vinegar. And although adding water to the vinegar does water it down or dilute it making it not so acidic, the resulting mixture of water and vinegar is still more than acidic enough to react with the baking soda. Also, adding warm water helps speed up the chemical reaction because it warms up everything else, especially the vinegar, and warmer reactants react together more quickly than cooler ones. The extra space the water takes up also means that not so much gas is needed to explode the bag.

The bag explodes because sooner or later the pressure of gas inside becomes too much for the bag to hold. Usually, the zip-lock is the place where the bag breaks but occasionally the zip-lock holds and the bag breaks open along an edge seam or somewhere else.

WHERE ON EARTH?

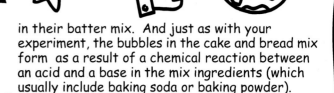

In your experiment you mixed an acid (vinegar) and a base (baking soda), which produced thick, bubbling foam full of carbon dioxide gas. These foaming gas bubbles inflated the bag and caused it to explode. Most cakes and breads inflate or rise as they bake because of similar bubbles forming in their batter mix. And just as with your experiment, the bubbles in the cake and bread mix form as a result of a chemical reaction between an acid and a base in the mix ingredients (which usually include baking soda or baking powder).

SOME TRICK TIPS!

- ...**Try different zip-lock bags-** some types and brands of zip-lock bag explode better than others.
- ...**Outdoors or in the bathroom-** because this experiment can get a bit messy (it's all part of the fun, you know!) I suggest you use the bathtub or better still outdoors, especially if you're not too keen on your house smelling like a fish-and-chips shop afterwards (it can get pretty smelly!).
- ...**Fiddly zip-locks-** some zip-locks can be a bit fiddly to zip up and if you don't really want to get covered in smelly vinegar foam you need to zip the bag closed before the fizzing gets out of control. One way of getting the zip done up even before the fizzing starts is to zip the bag halfway closed (as suggested in step 4 earlier), carefully put the packet of baking soda into the mouth of the bag and hold it up out of the vinegar by pinching it in place through the sides of the bag. Then simply zip the bag closed and release the packet to drop it into the vinegar.

ANSWERS TO SOME OF THE NUMBERED QUESTIONS:

ANS. 2: Wrapping the baking soda in a piece of paper towel or tissue means that it takes longer for it to react with the vinegar. You can think of it as a time release bag, because it takes more time to react than putting the powder straight into the vinegar without a wrapping. It takes more time for two main reasons. One is that it takes time for the vinegar to soak through the paper tissue and into the baking powder. The other reason is that wrapping the powder helps to keep it held together as one bigger more solid lump. A more solid lump of baking soda takes longer to react than a less solid, or more loosely packed same amount of baking soda. This is because the more solid lump has less surface area of baking powder in direct contact with the vinegar. If you break apart and separate the more solid lump into a collection of smaller lumps, there will be more surface area of the baking soda in contact with the vinegar. And remember that the baking powder needs to be in direct contact with the vinegar for a chemical reaction to take place.

ANS. 8: Other things you could change and explore include:
- ...Changing the temperature of the vinegar and/or the water;
- ...Trying different size zip-lock bags;
- ...Trying different types and brands of bags;
- ...Different types of paper tissue.

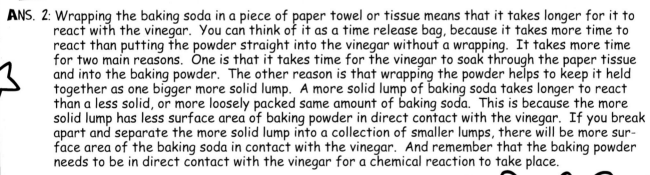

ANS. 9: Here's one suggestion on how to make a self-inflating balloon:
1. Pour some vinegar and water into a small bottle that has a narrow neck opening.
2. Using your small funnel, pour some baking soda into a balloon.
3. Carefully stretch the mouth of the balloon over the neck of the bottle, making sure it fits tightly (make sure the rest of the balloon dangles down the side of the bottle so that no baking soda can fall out).
4. Lift the balloon upright to drop the baking soda out and into the vinegar and water in the bottle.
5. The baking powder will react with the vinegar producing carbon dioxide gas, which will inflate the balloon!

And I'm quite sure that you can think of some other experiments you can do with this arrangement too!

© Dr Mark Biddiss 2001, 2005, 2011, Magical Science Book 1 @ www.Dr-Mark.co.uk

OBEDIENT SQUIRTY BOTTLE

OBJECTIVE: To have fun exploring how to apparently magically start and stop streams of water squirting from a bottle (preferably over somebody else!).

WANTED GROWN-UP HELP

SOME OF THE SCIENCE YOU'RE EXPLORING: Physics: Physical Processes: forces & motion, gravity, weight, force & pressure, atmospheric pressure, Chemistry: Properties of materials: liquids & gases, surface tension.

WHAT YOU NEED: An empty plastic fizzy-drink bottle (up to 1 litre) with the screw-on cap, a very thin pin (or nail) and some pliers.

1 WITH A GROWN-UP'S HELP grip the back end of your thin pin (or nail) with the pliers and firmly but CAREFULLY use the point of the pin to pierce three or four tiny holes around the bottom of the plastic bottle.

2 Stand the bottle and hold it firmly in some shallow water in a bowl or the sink, making sure the water is deep enough to be above the holes you just made. While still standing the bottle in the bowl or sink, fill it to the top with water.

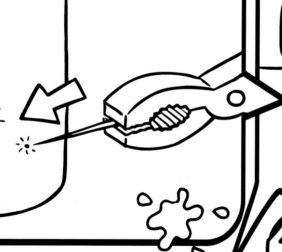

3 Holding the bottle near the neck opening, slowly lift it up above the water and hold it there steady for a few seconds.

4 While still holding the bottle steadily above the water, use your other hand to carefully screw on the cap tightly.

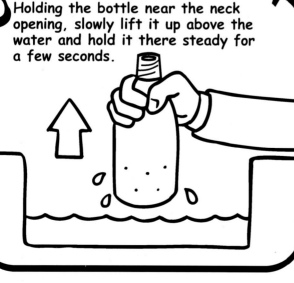

© Dr Mark Biddiss 2001, 2005, 2011, Magical Science Book 1 @ www.Dr-Mark.co.uk

WHAT HAPPENS?

When you lift the bottle from the water in the sink and hold it steadily in the air, streams of water leak from the holes you made. When you screw the cap on tightly, water quickly stops coming out from the holes.

SOME QUESTIONS TO THINK ABOUT

1. What do you think is going on? (see SO WHATS GOING ON?)
2. What happens if you unscrew the cap again?
3. What happens if you squeeze the bottle around its widest part, say, around the middle? (explanation provided)
4. What other things (variables) could you change to explore what happens? (some suggestions provided)

(Numbered answers and explanations to some of the questions are given on the next page)

SO WHAT'S GOING ON?

With no cap on the bottle, air pushes down on the surface of the water inside through the bottleneck opening. While you are filling the bottle, the water can't leak from the holes you made because they are underwater. The water outside the bottle, plus the force of the air pushing down on it from above (air pressure) pushes back against the holes and prevents the water inside from escaping. The water escapes from the holes when you lift the bottle above the water because now there is no water outside to stop it and the air pressure outside alone is just not enough. Now the combined force from the weight of the water inside the bottle and the air pressure pushing down on its surface from above are together strong enough to force the water out through the holes. As the water level in the bottle goes down, more air is drawn in through the open mouth of the bottle and continues to push down on the water, which helps to continually force it out through the holes.

There are two main reasons that the water stops flowing when you screw the cap tightly onto the bottle:

1. Now the combined forces from the weight of the water and the air trapped inside the bottle are together NOT strong enough to force the water out through the holes. This is because there is slightly less water in the bottle, but mainly because replacing the cap stops the air pressure from outside pushing down on the top of the water in the bottle. In other words, the combined downward force from the water and the air sealed in the bottle is now much less than the pressure of the air outside of the bottle, which is pushing to stop the water from leaking from the holes.

2. Water particles or molecules pull on each other to stick together. Water molecules at the surface (between water and air) have no water molecules to pull against on the air side. So to make up for this they pull more strongly against the other molecules next to them. This helps to form a strong surface layer that behaves like a stretchy skin and is called the meniscus. The pull from the water molecules that forms this stretchy meniscus skin is called surface tension. The surface tension in the tiny meniscus skin of the water at each hole in the bottle is strong enough, with the push of the air from outside, to stop the rest of the water from inside the bottle leaking through.

So, to sum up, the combined force of the greater air pressure outside the bottle and the strength of the tiny watery meniscus skin at each hole, is enough to keep the water in the bottle.

WHERE ON EARTH?

Some people store and carry water in bags or bottles made from thick cloth. This cloth has loads of tiny gaps or holes between the cloth fibre strands. The water doesn't leak very much through these tiny holes because of the surface tension in the tiny meniscus skin of water at each hole (just the same as with the holes in your bottle). The cloth in umbrellas and tents also stops the rain coming through in the same way; so as the cloth gets wet, it keeps you dry!

SOME TRICK TIPS!

- ...**Can get messy** - careful where you do this experiment because things can get a bit wet!

- ...**Melt bigger holes**, BUT BE CAREFUL! - To make holes with larger pins or nails, you may find it easier to get the nail or pin very hot in a flame or on the cooking stove and melt each hole in the plastic bottle.

ANSWERS TO SOME OF THE NUMBERED QUESTIONS:

ANS. 3: While you hold the bottle by the cap you are not affecting the forces either inside or outside the bottle and no water comes out from the holes. When you hold the bottle, say, around the middle (or hand the bottle to someone else to hold TEE-HEE!), the water will immediately start to leak from the holes (all over someone else, with any luck!). To hold the bottle without it slipping from your fingers you will be squeezing it slightly. This will increase the pressure of the air and water inside the bottle just enough to overcome the pressure from the air outside and also overcome the surface tension of the watery meniscus skin at the holes trying to hold the water in. Thus, the water streams out from the holes!

ANS. 4: Other things you could change and explore include:

...Trying different size bottles;

...Try the same experiment but with more holes around the bottom of the bottle;

...Try the same experiment but with a few more tiny holes further up the bottle, say, three around the middle and three nearer the top;

...Try the same experiment with a new bottle and make three or four holes around the bottom as you did in step 2 earlier, but this time use a much fatter nail.

12. MAGNETIC HANDS & WEIGHTLESS ARMS

OBJECTIVE:
To have fun exploring how to make your hands feel like repelling magnets and how to make your arms feel almost weightless.

WHAT YOU NEED:
A friend who is at least as strong as you are in their arms and shoulders. (These experiments can be done on your own but they're easier to do if you can find a friend to help).

SOME OF THE SCIENCE YOU'RE EXPLORING:
Biology: Ourselves, muscles & movement, nervous system, sense illusions, forces & motion.

1 Face your friend and keeping your elbows tucked in against the sides of your body, hold your hands straight out in front as if you're about to start clapping. You need your arms to be bent in an L-shape at your elbows and the palms of your hands facing each other. You should start with your hands about 15 to 20cm apart. Ask your friend to face you with their hands and arms in the same position.

2 Get them to stand close enough so that they can rest their palms against the back of your hands. The back of your right hand should be touching the palm of their left hand and the back of your left hand should be touching the palm of their right hand. With all hands in place, you need to push outwards against your friends hands as hard as you can and they must try hard to push inwards to stop your hands from moving. Remember to keep your elbows tucked in at your sides at all times. Continue this hard pushing without resting for an instant for about one minute if you can, or otherwise for as long as possible.

3 After about one minute or when you just can't push hard any longer, both you and your friend must stop pushing altogether and RELAX your arm muscles, and ask your friend to take their hands from yours. Now VERY GENTLY AND SLOWLY swing your hands together, back and forth as if clapping in slow motion.

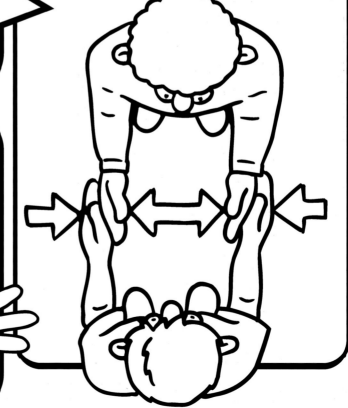

© Dr Mark Biddiss 2001, 2005, 2011, Magical Science Book 1 @ www.Dr-Mark.co.uk

WHAT HAPPENS?

If all goes well, it will feel as if there is an invisible force field actually between the palms of your hands, which tries gently to push your hands apart every time they swing very close together, a bit like repelling magnets. Otherwise it may feel as though your arms have become very light in weight and want to swing open almost by themselves. These feelings or sensations will only last for a few seconds.

SOME QUESTIONS TO THINK ABOUT

1. What do you think is going on?   (see 'SO WHAT'S GOING ON?')
2. How does it feel if you don't push outwards continuously, but rather keep stopping and starting again?
3. How does it feel when you repeat this experiment but push outwards hard with just one hand only?
4. How does it feel if your friend keeps your hands closer together or further apart as you push outwards?
5. How do you think you could do a similar experiment to make your whole straightened arm, or both straightened arms feel almost weightless and even swing upwards on their own? (suggestion provided)
6. How could you do these experiments on your own, without a friend's help? (suggestion provided)

(Numbered answers and explanations to some of the questions are given on the next page)

SO WHAT'S GOING ON?

Movement of your arms and legs (and other parts of your body too) is caused by some of the muscles there pulling, or contracting, while other opposing muscles relax. So even when it feels like you're pushing outwards with your hands, that pushing is actually caused by muscles in your arm and around your shoulders pulling or contracting. So rather than pushing outwards, you're really pulling your hands wider apart.

When you want to push outwards against your friend's hands, a nerve signal is sent from your brain and central nervous system to nerves in the muscles concerned and makes them contract by a chemical process. As you continue to push hard outwards, so too does the load continue on your contracting arm and shoulder muscles. Monitoring systems in these muscles sense the continuing load and send signals to your central nervous system and to your brain. Return signals run back to the nerves in the muscles and tell them to keep contracting. When you stop pushing and relax, the load on your contracting arm and shoulder muscles suddenly decreases. The return nerve signal, or stimulus, has now stopped which caused the muscles to contract, but the chemical processes it started within the muscles to cause contraction continues for a short time. Thus the muscles have a tendency to want to continue contracting and pull the hands apart, even when you're trying to relax the muscles and gently swing your hands together using different pulling muscles. We are not used to our arms trying to move by themselves and so we can be left with the illusion that an external or outside force is pushing them apart.

WHERE ON EARTH?

The weightless or less heavy feeling you will hopefully get in your arms is the same as that felt by anyone who carries out an activity where they need to use their muscles to push or pull continuously in the same direction for a long period of time. For example, people who spend a long time carrying heavy loads on their backs, such as someone walking and carrying a heavy backpack, feel very light in weight if they walk around for a minute or so immediately after taking the heavy pack off their back.

SOME TRICK TIPS!

- ...**Keep elbows tucked in at all times**- it's important for the success of the magnetic hands experiment.
- ...**Make sure your friend keeps your hands still**- make sure your friend is strong enough to stop your hands from pushing outwards and getting further apart.
- ...**Push constantly**- and don't keep stopping and starting if you want to feel the force.
- ...**No pain, no gain**- don't worry if your muscles begin to ache while pushing; that's actually a good sign that you're pushing properly (and a sign that your muscle fibres are tearing apart, but not to worry!).
- ...**Not too much** - If you repeat this experiment too many times you will probably find your muscles aching for the rest of the day while the damage you've done is being repaired, but not to worry!
- ...**Relax for a few minutes between experiments**- this gives your muscles a chance to get back to normal.

ANSWERS TO SOME OF THE NUMBERED QUESTIONS:

ANS. 5: Here's one experiment where you could try to make both straightened arms feel very light or even weightless:

1. Stand with your arms straight down at your sides, elbows locked.
2. Ask a friend to hold your wrists tightly against your body while you try to swing your arms upwards and outwards (like flapping wings). Lock your elbows and keep your arms straight at all times. Keep on pushing without resting for an instant for about one minute if you can, or otherwise for as long as possible.
3. After about one minute, or when you just can't push hard any longer, ask your friend to let go of your wrists. Relax as completely as you can and VERY GENTLY start to swing your arms up.

If all goes well it should feel as though your arms have become very light in weight or they may even float upwards on their own! That floating feeling is what your whole body would feel like up in space!

ANS. 6: To do these experiments on your own without a friend you will need something else to push against. For example, in the experiment suggested in answer 5 above, you could stand in a narrow doorway with the door open and try to swing your arms upwards and outwards against the doorframe. After a minute or so of pushing hard, simply step forward or backwards out of the doorway and complete step 3 above. Another way might be to wear some trousers with deep enough pockets to put your hands in while keeping your arms straight. Just be careful that you don't split your trousers!

And I'm sure that you can think of other ways.

FIRE-RAISING & SUCKING GLASSES

13

OBJECTIVE:
To have fun exploring how heat causes water to rise and how it can stick glasses to tables.

DANGER GROWN-UP HELP NEEDED

WHAT YOU NEED:
Small candle (preferably one that can float - night-light candles are good), a bowl (at least 2 or 3cm deep and preferably see-through), see-through glass jar or beaker (the narrower the better), water, modeling clay or putty and matches (or lighter).

SOME OF THE SCIENCE YOU'RE EXPLORING:
Chemistry & Physics: Properties of Materials, burning materials, liquids & gases, density, temperature & materials, physical changes, non-reversible changes, Physical Processes: Forces & motion & pressure.

1 Stick three or four small blobs of modelling putty around the rim edge of your glass jar. (The blobs of putty need to be secured and evenly spaced around the rim so that they can support and hold the rim of the upturned jar just one or two millimetres up off the bottom of the bowl.

2 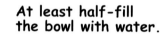 At least half-fill the bowl with water.

3 Gently place your candle so that it floats in the centre of the bowl of water (see 'SOME TRICK TIPS' for a suggestion on how to fix a candle that doesn't float).

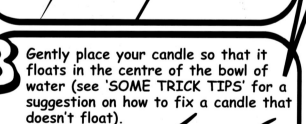

4 Ask a grown-up to light the candle with a match (or lighter) and then gently lower the upturned jar down over the burning candle and down into the water, so that the rim of the jar is well below the surface of the water and comes to rest on the bottom of the bowl on the blobs of putty you placed around the rim.

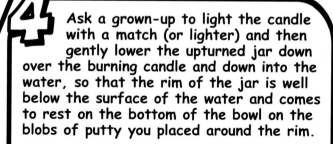

WHAT HAPPENS?

As you lower the jar down over the burning candle and into the water, you should notice the level of the water inside the jar is pushed down below the level of the water outside surrounding the jar. You may also see a few tiny bubbles escaping from around the rim of the jar. As you watch, the candle continues burning and the water level inside the jar very slowly begins to rise again. Very soon, the candle begins to flicker and then goes out completely quite quickly and during this time there is a more rapid rise in water level inside the jar. You should notice the water level continues to rise much more slowly again for a short time after the candle has burned out.

SOME QUESTIONS TO THINK ABOUT

1. What do you think is going on? (see 'SO WHAT'S GOING ON?')
2. What happens if you use two or more candles? (see 'SOME TRICK TIPS' on how and answer provided)
3. What other things (variables) could you change to explore what happens? (some suggestions provided)

(Numbered answers and explanations to some of the questions are given on the next page)

SO WHAT'S GOING ON?

As you lower the jar down over the candle, even before it goes down into the water, the candle flame burns using the oxygen in the air (in combustion) and heats up the air around it and the air trapped above within the jar. Because the air in the jar expands as it heats up, some of it will be forced out because there's not enough room. So even before the rim of your jar goes down below the water level, you have lost some air from inside due to expansion. As the rim of the jar goes down into the water, the air inside becomes trapped and sealed in, and has enough pressure to push the level of the water down inside the jar below that of the water outside. The tiny bubbles you may see coming out from around the rim of the jar are due to the continuing expansion of the air inside as it heats up a little more.

For a few seconds after the jar has been placed down, the candle flame continues to burn steadily as it uses up oxygen from the air in the jar. As the oxygen is being used up, there is a drop in pressure (or suction effect) because the air that's left doesn't need so much room. Now the air pressure inside the glass is less than that of the air outside. The greater pressure of air on the water outside the glass causes the water level inside to be pushed up and rise just a little and very slowly to fill the gap left by the oxygen. However, the candle flame very soon starts to flicker and then goes out completely because the oxygen level in the air in the jar gets too low to keep the flame burning hot enough. As the flame flickers low and goes out completely, there is a sudden drop in the temperature of the air in the jar. This causes the air to contract quickly, which causes a sudden and bigger drop in pressure than before (or bigger suction), and this causes the water to rise up much higher and at a faster rate than before. The water level continues to rise just a little and much more slowly again immediately after the flame has gone out because the air is still cooling and so contracting, but at a much slower rate.

WHERE ON EARTH?

One example you can see easily is on the draining surface next to your kitchen sink, especially if the surface is smooth and any drainage groves or channels aren't too deep. When people wash drinking glasses in hot water, they often place them upturned on the flat drainage surface next to the sink to allow much of the water to drain off and out of the glass before being dried completely. If there is a lot of water on the draining surface, what often happens is that water flows around the rim of the upturned glass and makes an airtight seal. Having been washed in hot water, the air trapped inside the glass started off quite warm and cools down while the glass is resting on the draining surface. As it cools down, it contracts and sucks water up into the glass, in the same way as it did with the cooling air in your experiment. When I've washed and placed hot drinking glasses in this way I frequently return a short time later to dry the glasses only to find a centimetre or so of water has been sucked up into the glass. Occasionally I've rested my upturned glasses on a much smoother surface on the other side of my sink only to return to find some of my glasses stuck down quite firmly!

SOME TRICK TIPS!

...**You can use candles that don't float**- all you need to do is fix them to the bottom of your bowl, perhaps using some of your modelling putty. Just make sure that they are tall enough to stick out and up above the surface of your water. You can use more than one candle - those very narrow birthday-cake candles work well. I either fix them on a floating candle or fix them directly to the bottom of the bowl.

ANSWERS TO SOME OF THE NUMBERED QUESTIONS:

ANS. 2: The more candles you burn, the higher the water level rises inside your jar (though I have to admit that I've never tried more than four candles at the same time). This is easily explained by the fact that burning more candles produces more heat. So, the hotter the air in the jar, the more it expands while it's being heated and so the more it contracts as it cools again. And the more it contracts, the lower the pressure (or greater the suction) and so more water flows up into the jar. You can also get the water to rise higher if you use a candle with a bigger flame, because it'll be hotter.

Incidentally, some sources say that the reason the water rises is because the oxygen is being used up by the burning candle and they generally say nothing about the cooling and contracting air effect. They say that the candle flame goes out because all the oxygen has been used up and that the volume of risen water in the jar is the same as the volume of oxygen burned by the candle. Unfortunately, this explanation is not quite correct and doesn't explain why burning more candles (or a bigger hotter flame) causes a greater rise in the water level or the fact that there is actually still some oxygen left even after the candle has gone out. As I hope has been made clear in my explanation, the rise due to oxygen consumption is actually very small and is in fact mostly due to the contraction of the cooling air in the jar.

ANS. 3: Other things you could change and explore include:
   ...Try using narrower or wider jars;
   ...Try using a fatter or thinner candle;
   ...Try using very hot or very cold water;
   ...Try using a very hot or very cold (from the ice box) jar;
   ...Try using thicker or more viscous liquids instead of water (such as treacle and oil).

⑭ MYSTERY OF THE MOVING EGG EGGSPERIMENT

OBJECTIVE: To have eggcitment and fun eggsperimenting and eggsploring the mystery of the moving egg (O-o-o-o-o-o-o-h-h-h!!) and how you can tell the difference between a raw and a hard-boiled egg without breaking the shell.

SOME OF THE SCIENCE YOU'RE EXPLORING:
Physics: Physical Processes, forces & motion, force & rotation, friction & air-resistance, gravity,
Chemistry: Properties of materials: solids & liquids, changing materials & eggology
(OK, OK, I made that last one up!)

WHAT YOU NEED: To eggsperience and eggsamine this eggstraordinary eggsperiment you'll need a raw egg, a cooked hard-boiled egg and a broad flat, smooth surface (such as a table top or smooth floor or even a dinner plate). (And I'll try to resist any more egg wordplay jokes OK!).

1 Take a raw egg and set it spinning quite fast on its side on the flat smooth surface.

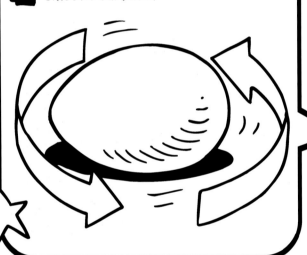

2 Press down on the spinning egg lightly with your fingers, but firmly enough to stop it spinning.

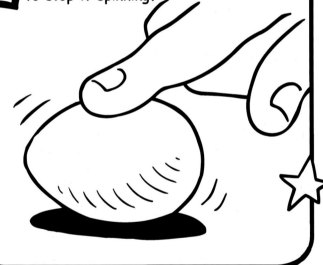

3 As soon as the egg stops spinning, IMMEDIATELTY lift your fingers away.

WHAT HAPPENS?

When you spin the raw egg you'll probably notice that it feels a little sluggish in getting going, as if it was somehow resisting the spin. It will also wobble at first as it spins. When you stop it spinning completely and immediately take your fingers away, the egg starts to spin slowly again in the same direction.

SOME QUESTIONS TO THINK ABOUT?

1. What do you think is going on? (see 'SO WHAT'S GOING ON ?' for an eggsplanation)
2. What happens if you do the same eggsperiment with a hard-boiled egg? (eggsplanation provided)
3. What other things (variables) could you change to explore what happens? (some suggestions provided)

(Numbered answers and explanations to some of the questions are given on the next page)

SO WHAT'S GOING ON?

First of all, there are a few important facts you need to keep in mind:

1. Inside a raw egg the contents are mostly liquid and so can flow about and move independently of the enclosing shell.

2. When you spin or stop an egg, you are spinning or stopping it by touching the shell; you are not actually touching what's inside the shell.

3. Something that is standing still wants to stay standing still and something that is moving wants to keep on moving in the same way (as stated in Isaac Newton's First Law of Motion).

This tendency of something to stay as it is (or to resist a change in its state of motion) is called inertia.

So, how do we eggsplain the mystery of the moving egg eggsperiment bearing these three facts in mind?

(OK I promise not to use any more stupid egg-words, alright?)

The raw egg feels somewhat sluggish when you first start to spin it because it takes a brief moment for the liquid contents to start spinning inside and catch up with the spin of the shell. The wobbling occurs because of the shape of the egg; rounded (or hemispherical) at one end and slightly more pointed at the other. This egg-shape causes an uneven circular flow of the slower (or faster) moving liquid contents as the egg spins and this causes the whole egg to wobble. When you press your fingers on the spinning raw egg to stop it, you stop the shell well enough. However, the inertia of the liquid contents inside the shell keeps the contents flowing in the same direction of spin for a short time. So if you let go of the shell again quickly enough, the liquid contents are still moving and make the egg as a whole start spinning slowly again, as the liquid flows around the inside surface of the shell, rubbing against it and dragging it around.

WHERE ON EARTH?

Your body relies on the behaviour of a liquid inside a moving container (as with your mysterious moving egg) to sense motion. As I'm sure you know, you can sense which way your head is moving and turning, without using your eyes. You sense this motion using two motion sensors, one deep inside of each ear chamber. Each sensor is made up of three looping tubes called semicircular canals. Each semicircular canal (or SCC for short) loops in a different direction. And each SCC is hollow and filled with liquid. At some point in the SCC tube it widens out, and in that chamber is a small flap called the capula. The capula is like a two-way swinging door and reaches right across the chamber. It is fixed and hinges on the outside edge of the SCC and completely seals the chamber, even when it swings either way. So the liquid can't flow right through the chamber.

Now here's how it all works: when you move and turn your head in any direction you also move and turn the semicircular canals (or SCCs) in your ears. The liquid inside of each SCC resists this motion and tries to stay where it is. So for a short time, the SCC and attached capula flap are moving and the liquid inside the SCC is not moving, or moving much more slowly. This causes the liquid to push against and swing the capula in one direction. The capula is packed with tiny hair cells. These cells send one kind of signal to your brain when your capula (or head) moves in one direction, and a different signal when it moves in the other direction. If your head (and SCC) keeps moving at the same speed and in the same direction, sooner or later the moving liquid catches up and stops pushing against and moving the capula. When the capula has stopped moving, it stops sending movement signals to your brain and you don't sense motion any longer. That's why it can feel like you're not moving in a vehicle (especially a train or aeroplane) that's moving at a constant velocity (same speed and direction). However, when the vehicle slows down rapidly, your body and head take a tiny bit longer to slow with it. That's how come you can feel that you're slowing down.

From all this can you now figure out why you feel dizzy and as though you're still moving if you spin around and around for a while and then suddenly stop?

SOME TRICK TIPS!

...You must let go of the raw egg immediately it stops spinning— if you don't the liquid inside may stop moving too before you let go and the egg won't start spinning again.

ANSWERS TO SOME OF THE NUMBERED QUESTIONS:

ANS. 2: A hard-boiled egg is solid throughout and so the whole egg (shell and contents) moves together as a solid object. Because of this you should notice the following things when you spin the hard-boiled egg: most obviously **1**: it doesn't start to spin slowly again when you stop it spinning and quickly remove your fingers. Remember that with a hard-boiled egg, when you stop the shell with your fingers you also stop the solid contents; so the egg wont continue to spin when you let go. **2** It doesn't feel sluggish when you start it spinning; it starts spinning more easily. Remember that the raw egg felt sluggish because of the slower moving fluid inside. **3** It doesn't wobble in quite the same way as it spins. Remember that the wobble in the raw egg was in part caused by the uneven flow of the slower or faster moving liquid inside the shell. **4** It spins faster and for longer than the raw egg (using the same spin force). In the raw egg the slower moving fluid acts like a brake on the surrounding shell as it rubs against it from the inside. So now you know some of the ways you can use to tell the difference between a raw and a hard-boiled egg without breaking the shell!

ANS. 3: Other things you could change and explore include:
   ...What happens if you start off by spinning the egg even faster or more slowly?
   ...Does it make any difference to the results if you spin the egg in the opposite direction?
   ...Does anything different happen if you try different size eggs?

15. TASTELESS TONGUE & APPLE-POTATOES

OBJECTIVE: To have fun exploring how your senses of taste and smell work together and how to trick your sense of flavour.

SOME OF THE SCIENCE YOU'RE EXPLORING: Biology: Ourselves: senses, taste, smell & flavour.

WHAT YOU NEED: Firstly, you will need at least three or four of the following raw foods: an apple, a potato, a carrot, a turnip, a pear and an onion (and make sure that they are all fresh, juicy and crisp). You will also need some plates, a sharp knife (or grater), some spoons or forks, a cup of drinking water and a friend.

1. Cut (or grate) some apple, potato, carrot, turnip and some pear (or at least three of these food items) into small pieces of about the same size. Clean your knife or grater each time you go to cut a different food item. Place each food separately on its own plate and with its own spoon or fork.

2. Close your eyes, squeeze and block your nostrils tightly closed (you should not be able to smell anything or breath through your nose), and ask your friend to feed you just a little of one of the foods without telling you which one it is.

3. Chew it for just a few seconds and try to taste which of the foods you are eating. Swallow it or spit it out.

Rinse your mouth with water, and ask your friend to feed you a different food. Repeat this until you have tasted all the foods

WHAT HAPPENS?

As long as you keep your eyes and nostrils tightly closed, the chances are that you will find it almost impossible to tell all the different foods apart, one from the other.

SOME QUESTIONS TO THINK ABOUT

1. What do you think is going on? (see 'SO WHAT'S GOING ON?')
2. What happens if you repeat the experiment with your eyes and nostrils fully open?
3. What happens if you try the first experiment with the food hot (**NOT** cooked) or very cold? (answer provided)
4. What other foods could you try? (suggestion provided)
5. Is there any difference in the results found between adults and children? (answer provided)
6. What sensation do you get if you chew, say, a piece of raw potato while sniffing strongly on a piece of fresh juicy apple held directly under your nose? Or chew apple while sniffing onion? (answer provided)

(Numbered answers and explanations to some of the questions are given on the next page)

SO WHAT'S GOING ON?

We usually distinguish different foods by their flavour and texture. Flavour is a combination of taste and smell.

Tasting is what your tongue does and is in a way the simplest of your senses. Your tongue can only taste bitter, salt, sour and sweet. Covering the back, front and each side of your tongue are thousands of tiny taste buds, or papillae, each specialising in one of the four basic tastes. The back of your tongue is where the taste buds for bitter are mostly grouped. Your salt taste buds are grouped mainly along each side of your tongue, towards the back, but with some on the tip of your tongue too. Your sour taste buds are grouped along each side of your tongue, towards the front. Sweetness, one of the most popular tastes (for some of us anyway!), can only be detected by a comparatively small group of taste buds right on the tip of your tongue.

Smelling is what your nose does and is several thousand times more sensitive to smells and odours than your tongue is to taste! Whereas your tongue can only tell the difference between four basic tastes, your nose can probably tell the difference between a few thousand different smells and odours! In fact, scientists reckon that a trained human sniffer can recognise up to about ten thousand different odours!
Phew!

Now, when we eat (or drink) something our less sensitive tongue senses the taste of the food and our more sensitive nose senses the smells or odours coming from it. So much of the distinctive flavour of many foods comes from the smells and odours they give off, particularly the foods in your experiment. The foods in your experiment also all have a similar texture (they are all similarly crisp and juicy). And since they all actually taste very similar too, the main difference in their flavours is in the odours they give off. So by holding your nostrils closed, you cannot easily sense the odours and so it seems that all five foods have the same flavour.

© Dr Mark Biddiss 2001, 2005, 2011, Magical Science Book 1 @ www.Dr-Mark.co.uk

WHERE ON EARTH?

Have you ever noticed how many different foods don't seem to have so much taste when you have a blocked nose because of a bad cold or flu? Well, many people have. In fact, lots of people also say that many of the foods they eat when they have a blocked nose taste very similar. Even I've noticed this. From your experiment you should be able to easily figure out the reason why. Also, when I was a little boy, whenever my mum gave me some horrible tasting medicine to take from a spoon, she would always tell me to squeeze my nostrils shut at the same time. And I still do the same thing when I occasionally take medicine even now I'm all grown-up, after all, are there really any nice tasting medicines? Not according to my taste, anyway!

SOME TRICK TIPS!

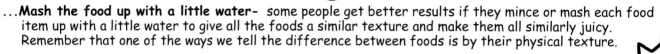

...**Mash the food up with a little water** - some people get better results if they mince or mash each food item up with a little water to give all the foods a similar texture and make them all similarly juicy. Remember that one of the ways we tell the difference between foods is by their physical texture.

...**And NO cheating either!** - to experience this experiment properly, you MUST keep your eyes and nostrils tightly closed all the time. Even a tiny peep or the slightest whiff of the food will probably give your brain all the clues it needs to tell which food you are chewing.

ANSWERS TO SOME OF THE NUMBERED QUESTIONS:

ANS. 3: Different temperatures change the way your taste buds work and how odours come off the food, so the flavour of food may also be affected by the foods temperature. You may notice this difference even with your nostrils closed. Most people say that sweet foods taste sweeter when they are warmer, while salty and bitter foods taste saltier and bitter, respectively, when colder. Sourness seems to be the least affected by temperature, you may not even notice the difference. Hotter foods may also give off more odours than colder foods, so making them easier to smell and give them a stronger flavour. Heating the food will also change its texture and this change happens most when the food is fully cooked. So try not to actually cook the food when you heat it.

ANS. 4: There are many other common, everyday foods that are almost impossible for many people to tell the difference between if they can't smell them as well as taste them. In other words, the flavour of these foods is also mostly due to the odours they give off. Examples of other such foods are said to be chocolate (YUM!), garlic, cherry, cranberry juice, apricot, molasses and pineapple. However, there are also many common, everyday foods that are much more easy to recognise without being able to smell them. Such foods include onion, lemon, sugar, salt, vinegar, sour cream, grapes, cheese, ketchup and mustard. Why not repeat your experiment with some of these various foods to see which ones you can easily identify without your sense of smell?

ANS. 5: There may well be a difference between the results of children and adults who do this experiment. Adults often find it even harder to tell the difference between the foods than children. The number of taste buds on your tongue changes throughout your life. Young babies have very few taste buds. Children actually have many more taste buds than adults. And adults actually loose more and more taste buds as they get older and older. All of this may help to explain at least part of the reason why your taste may change as you get older. There are some foods you may like as a child that you don't like when you grow up (and the other way around of course).

ANS. 6: If you chew a piece of raw potato while at the same time sniffing a fresh and juicy piece of apple, there's a good chance that it'll seem like you're eating apple-flavoured potato (or maybe potato-flavoured apple)! And if you chew a piece of apple while sniffing a piece of onion, well, YUK! onion-flavoured apple (or apple-flavoured onion)! Of course, YOU may actually like the taste!

16. BOUNCIN' BLUBBER BALLS & POTTY PUTTY

OBJECTIVE:
To have fun exploring a fun and easy (and messy) way of making a rubbery, bouncy plastic material.

WARNING: MESSY EXPERIMENT & DON'T EAT THE MATERIALS (THEY ARE NOT POISONOUS BUT COULD STILL BE HARMFUL)

WHAT YOU NEED:
Some water soluble (or washable) white PVA glue, borax powder (a natural general-purpose household cleaner), some water, a measuring jug, a large spoon (or tablespoon), and some food dye (optional). You might also want to put down some old newspaper or plastic to protect your work surfaces.

SOME OF THE SCIENCE YOU'RE EXPLORING:
Chemistry: Properties of Materials: different materials, solids & liquids, chemical reactions, chemical & physical change, plastics & polymers; Physics: Physical Processes: forces & motion.

1. Put 1 heaped tablespoon of borax powder into a measuring jug and add about 300ml of water. Stir well for a few seconds to dissolve the borax powder into the water and until it looks white and cloudy. Leave this to stand still for a few minutes until the water clears and you should see some un-dissolved borax powder in the bottom of the jug.

2. Now pour about 2 tablespoons of white PVA glue slowly into the borax-water mixture. A stringy glob of white plastic material will immediately form floating in the borax solution.

3. Quickly reach into the jug and lift out as much of the glob as you can. It will feel very, very, stringy, gooey, soft and slippery! This will get less so as you handle it. Gently squeeze, slide and roll the glob from one hand to the other try not to fold it. You may find it less slippery to hold and move around if you wash the glob and your hands under tap water once or twice while you roll it around from hand to hand. Also, stopping briefly to dry your hands and then continuing with the rolling can also help to dry the glob a little and make it easier to handle. Keep rolling for a few minutes until the glob holds as a ball.

4. Now gently throw your white blubbery ball onto a hard, smooth, flat surface (such as wall, floor or table-top) and see what happens. Then perhaps throw it harder.

© Dr Mark Biddiss 2001, 2005, 2011, Magical Science Book 1 @ www.Dr-Mark.co.uk

You have a bouncin' blubber ball just like a bouncin' rubber ball!

SOME QUESTIONS TO THINK ABOUT

1. What do you think is going on? (see 'SO WHAT'S GOING ON?')
2. What happens if you grip a piece of blubber with both hands and first VERY SLOWLY pull the ends in opposite directions, and then QUICKLY pull them in opposite directions? (answer provided)
3. What happens if you leave a blubber ball on some newspaper on a flat kitchen surface (answer provided)
4. Can you think of a way of making blubber just in your hands without bowls or spoons? (answer provided)
5. What other things (variables) could you change to explore what happens? (some suggestions provided)

(Numbered answers and explanations to the questions are given on the next page)

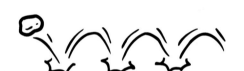

SO WHAT'S GOING ON?

Almost everything is made from particles called molecules. Plastic molecules, or polymers, are giant, flexible molecules made up of long chains of thousands of smaller molecules (called monomers).

White PVA glue is made up of millions of polymer chains. In the glue these polymer chains are dissolved in water and they slide around each other. This allows the glue to flow like a liquid. But because these polymers chains are so long and there are so many, they get in each other's way which makes the glue thicker, or more viscous, and flow more slowly than water.

When you add a borax-water solution to PVA glue, you cause a chemical reaction. The borax molecules cross-link, connect and bind up the glue polymer chains. This causes the chains to link and tangle together side by side and cross over each other - a bit like the strands of a tangled fishing net. The glue polymer chains cannot now move as freely and independently of each other as they did before. This means that the glue-borax mix as a whole can no longer flow or pour as easily and freely as it did before. It has become more viscous. Also, the more the glue polymer chains are linked and tangle, the more water they trap. This gives your material a jelly-like feel.

So you end up with a new plastic material which is the result of a chemical reaction between borax-water solution and PVA glue. And it has some rather interesting properties unlike the original glue or borax solution ingredients. The long, tangled polymer chains that make up your new material (as well as rubber and many plastics) are called elastomers. These elastomers are what make these materials flexible and, well, elastic! Being elastic means that it can spring back to its original shape after being slightly squashed, stretched or squeezed. In its ball-shape, when the ball hits the surface the force of impact causes the ball to flatten slightly. But it quickly returns to its original ball-shape, causing it to re-bound and push off the surface. The more quickly it returns to its original shape, the higher it bounces.

WHERE ON EARTH?

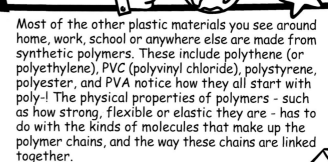

Borax is short for sodium tetraborate decahydrate, and PVA (or PVAc) is short for polyvinyl acetate - now you see why we like shortening scientific names! Borax is a general purpose household cleaner and white PVA glue is a general purpose household adhesive and sealer. Your PVA-borax bouncin' blubber plastic material is similar to plastic materials found all over the world. Polymers may be natural or man-made (synthetic). Wood, wool, rubber, starch and even your own hair and DNA, are examples of where you'll find natural polymers.

Most of the other plastic materials you see around home, work, school or anywhere else are made from synthetic polymers. These include polythene (or polyethylene), PVC (polyvinyl chloride), polystyrene, polyester, and PVA notice how they all start with poly-! The physical properties of polymers - such as how strong, flexible or elastic they are - has to do with the kinds of molecules that make up the polymer chains, and the way these chains are linked together.

SOME TRICK TIPS!

- ...**Keeping your bouncin' blubber when you finished playing** - oops! I mean, experimenting, you can keep your blubbery plastic for up to a few weeks by sealing it inside an air-tight bag or container.
- ...**Don't just leave it anywhere**- especially not on furniture, carpets or clothes. Leaving it on plastic is OK.
- ...**Wash hands thoroughly after**- the materials aren't poisonous but they could still make you ill if eaten.
- ...**Squirt PVA glue from a squeezy bottle**- the glue comes out in a thin stream and mixes better and more quickly in the borax solution.
- ...**Make bigger bowls of borax solution** for bouncin' blubber parties, e.g. 3 or 4 heaped tablespoons of borax powder into a bowl with about 1 litre of water. This can make it easier if you have lots of people who want to have a go at making their own bouncin' blubber. As one person takes their blubber out of the borax solution, just pour in a little more PVA glue for the next person. This works well for classes of pupils too!
- ...**Add food colouring to the PVA glue**- this is good if you want to make colourful bouncin blubber!

ANSWERS TO SOME OF THE NUMBERED QUESTIONS:

ANS. 2: Pull it very slowly in opposite directions and your piece of blubber will flow and stretch. Pull it apart quickly and your blubber will snap and tear in two! Pulling slowly allows time for the polymer chains to move and flow a little with you. Pull quickly and they don't have enough time and so snap. And once snapped, you won't be able to stick the pieces straight back together again. But they will still be able to bounce around OK.

ANS. 3: If you leave your blubber ball on a flat surface it will very very slowly collapse and flatten out. Although your blubber seems to be a bouncy solid, it is in fact a fluid. It just takes some time for it to flow. If you leave it on newspaper to flatten out and then peel it off again, you'll probably find a reverse copy of the newspaper print on the underside of your blubber. The blubber is still pretty moist and sticky, and the print of many newspapers and magazines can stick to it. So now you've got printing putty! How well your putty prints will depend upon the amounts of ingredients you use.

ANS. 4: First make your hands dripping wet. Next pour a small amount of PVA glue into the palm of one hand. Then add a pinch of borax powder (about a quarter of a teaspoon). Now you rub your wet palms and hands together around the glob of PVA and borax to mix it all together to make blubber!

ANS. 5: Other things you could change and explore include:
- ...Make a few different size blubber balls and test their bouncin' properties;
- ...Try mixing equal amounts of borax solution and PVA glue in a cup;
- ...Mix equal amounts of PVA glue and water together before pouring it into the borax solution;
- ...Make the borax solution with less or more borax powder (e.g. 1 heaped teaspoon with 300ml water)
- ...Try different brands and types of PVA white glue.
- ...Try pressing a big glob of blubber into a small pot to see if you can make a rude noise!

© Dr Mark Biddiss 2001, 2005, 2011, Magical Science Book 1 @ www.Dr-Mark.co.uk

BALLOON KEBABS & WATER-BAG PORCUPINES

OBJECTIVE: To have fun exploring how to spear a balloon and plastic bag full of water, without either bursting.

SOME OF THE SCIENCE YOU'RE EXPLORING: Chemistry & Physics: Properties of materials: liquids & solids, surface tension, polymers, physical changes, temperature & materials; Physical Processes: forces & motion, pushing & pulling, and force & pressure.

WHAT YOU NEED: A few round balloons, a polythene plastic freezer or sandwich bag (preferably see-through - zip-lock bags are good), some water, sharp toothpicks or cocktail-sticks, sharp wooden barbeque skewer sticks, several sharpened pencils, and a little cooking oil or washing-up liquid (or other liquid lubricant).

1 Inflate a balloon as fully as possible, hold it inflated for a minute or so, and then let it deflate and go down flat again. Fully inflate it a second time and then let it deflate until it is about half or two-thirds full of air. Tie a knot in the mouth end of the balloon to stop it deflating any more.

2 Dip the sharp pointed tip of a toothpick (or cocktail stick) in some cooking oil and push it very gently against the darker area of rubber opposite the tied end of the balloon.

3 Spin the toothpick by rotating it back and forth between your fingers. At the same time, very gently and slowly begin to push the spinning toothpick into the balloon. Keep on pushing and spinning until the pointed tip of the toothpick pierces through the balloons surface.

© Dr Mark Biddiss 2001, 2005, 2011, Magical Science Book 1 @ www.Dr-Mark.co.uk

WHAT HAPPENS?

If all goes to plan, and perhaps with a little practice, you should be able to pierce through the end of the balloon without popping it! You'll even be able to leave the toothpick in place without the balloon popping or deflating!

SOME QUESTIONS TO THINK ABOUT

1. What do you think is going on? (see 'SO WHAT'S GOING ON?')
2. Can you do this science trick with a fully inflated balloon? (answer provided)
3. Can you pierce the balloon with the toothpick, without popping it, through any other part of the balloon? (answer provided)
4. What happens if you carefully remove the toothpick and try to replace it, using the same tiny hole you made, with a fatter and longer wooden skewer coated in cooking oil? (answer provided)
5. Can you push the spinning skewer right the way through the balloon until it comes out the other side next to the knot, without the balloon popping? (answer provided)
6. Can you pierce and spear the balloon straight away using the skewer, without using a toothpick to make a hole first? (answer provided)
7. What happens if you try to push and spin a skewer or very sharp pencil into (or even right the way through) the sides of a polythene plastic sandwich or freezer bag filled with water? (answer provided)

(Numbered answers and explanations to some of the questions are given on the next page)

SO WHAT'S GOING ON?

Balloons are made of rubber, which is a stretchy polymer material. Rubber is made of tiny particles, or molecules, that are linked in long chains. These long chains of rubber molecules are linked and layered in a criss-cross or crosswise pattern, similar to the mesh screening you get in some oven doors. This crosswise pattern gives the rubber its stretchy quality. When you very slowly push your spinning toothpick into the balloon, it pushes some of the chains of rubber molecules apart slightly. This allows a tiny gap for your toothpick to slide in between and through the molecule chains, until it eventually comes out on the inside surface of the balloon. In fact, as long as your balloon isn't blown up too much, the rubber will actually tighten around the toothpick as it passes through! That's why your balloon doesn't deflate easily if you leave the toothpick in place. When you blow up the balloon completely and let it down again, you stretch and slightly weaken the rubber molecule chains. This makes it easier for the toothpick to pass through without damaging them. The cooking oil on your toothpick makes it more slippery and this reduces the friction, or gripping force, between the spinning toothpick and the rubber, and this also allows the toothpick to pass through the rubber more easily. Finally, the darker rubber through which you pushed your toothpick is darker because it hasnt been as stretched as the rest of the rubber of the balloon, and that leaves it slightly thicker too. Being less stretched and thicker makes it stronger and so less likely to split, causing the balloon to pop!

© Dr Mark Biddiss 2001, 2005, 2011, Magical Science Book 1 @ www.Dr-Mark.co.uk

WHERE ON EARTH?

The ability of some rubber and plastic polymer materials to grip and seal tightly around a thin piercing object is useful in vehicle tyres and the tops of bottles of liquid drugs made for syringes. When a nail pierces through a vehicle tyre, the rubber often grips tightly around the nail and helps prevent air from escaping so easily. With the bottles of liquid drugs for syringes, when the needle passes through the rubber material on the lid, a similar thing occurs as with the tyre. However, when the needle is removed, the rubber material contracts so much around the hole made by the needle that it actually closes the hole completely, preventing any liquid escaping from the bottle.

SOME TRICK TIPS!

- ... **Practice** - you might need to practice and try a few times before you get the toothpick and skewer through the balloon without popping it. So keep at it if you don't get it right first time, it's worth it!
- ... **Sharp points** - make sure that all of your toothpicks, wooden skewers and pencils are smooth and sharp, having cone-shape points rather than flattened blade-shape points, with no edges or ridges.
- ... **More oil** - if you don't succeed first time with the balloon, try using a little more cooking oil lubricant.

ANSWERS TO SOME OF THE NUMBERED QUESTIONS:

ANS. 2: NO! (Well, at least I've never been able to!) When the balloon is fully inflated, the rubber is being stretched pretty much to its limits and is likely to be as thin and as weak as it gets without tearing. Even the slightest damage to the rubber will cause it to split open.

ANS. 3: The only other place on the balloon where I've been able to easily pierce through the balloon without popping it is next to the knot, where the rubber is not so stretched.

ANS. 4: WITH SOME CARE, you should be able to remove the toothpick and insert an oiled wooden skewer back through the same hole without popping the balloon.

ANS. 5: YES! Again, WITH SOME CARE, you should be able to continue gently spinning and pushing the oiled skewer right the way through the balloon and out the other side next to the knot, just like a balloon kebab! It looks very impressive!

ANS. 6: YES! But this does take some practice and skill, not to mention a very sharp skewer and lots of cooking oil! Just repeat the whole experiment using a skewer instead of a toothpick.

ANS. 7: With just a little care and using the same technique you used with the balloon, you should very easily be able to push a skewer or sharp pencil into and right the way through a plastic bag filled with water without the bag tearing or the water leaking out! You can actually pierce the bag with several skewers or pencils at the same time, making a water-bag porcupine! Most sandwich and freezer bags are made of polythene (or polyethylene). Polythene shrinks and grips particularly well around any piercing objects, such as skewers and even fatter pencils, and this helps to stop the water from leaking out. Another reason that it doesn't easily leak is that the surface tension of the water keeps it from leaking out through the tiny gaps between the skewer (or pencil) and the plastic (see 'SO WHAT'S GOING ON' in experiment 11, **OBEDIENT SQUIRTY BOTTLE**, for a fuller explanation of this surface tension phenomenon).

18. WHITE GHOSTS & SPECTRAL SPECTRES

OBJECTIVE: To have fun exploring how to trick your eyes and brain into seeing ghostly black, white and colour images that are not really there.

WHAT YOU NEED: Some assorted colour pens or pencils, including a deep black pen (rather than a washed out black or dark grey), some sheets of blank white paper and some additional sheets of a selection of different colours, and a bright light source (bright daylight or a desk lamp).

SOME OF THE SCIENCE YOU'RE EXPLORING: Biology & Physics: Ourselves: senses, vision & seeing, perception, Physical Processes: Light & Colour.

1 Hold this book at arms length in front of you with a bright light shining on this page (such as in bright daylight or under a desk lamp) and stare hard into the white mouth of the ghostly black figure below for about 30 seconds. Make sure that you stare at the same place in the centre of the ghost for the whole time.

2 After 30 seconds or so of staring at the ghostly figure (the longer the better), immediately switch your stare into the middle of the spooky graveyard scene below and blink quickly.

WHAT HAPPENS?

When you stare at the graveyard scene you should see a whitish ghostly image floating amongst the graves.

SOME QUESTIONS TO THINK ABOUT

1. What do you think is going on? (see 'SO WHAT'S GOING ON?')
2. What happens if you repeat the experiment but instead use a coloured copy of the black ghost picture below, such as a bright red, blue, yellow and/or green ghost. (answer provided)
3. What other things (variables) could you change to explore what happens? (some suggestions provided)

(Numbered answers and explanations to the questions are given on the next page)

SO WHAT'S GOING ON?

When you look at anything, light from the scene you are looking at shines deep into each eye and onto the surface at the back. This inside back surface is called the retina and is covered in about 130 million tiny light detectors! About 122 million of theses light detectors are called rods and can only detect black and white, and can work well in very dim light. The rods cannot detect colour. However, there are also about 8 million of the light detectors called cones, and these do detect colour and also allow us to see things clearly focused. Now, when you stared hard at the black ghostly figure, the back central part of your retina on which the black image formed did not receive any bright light (because black can be thought of as a lack or absence of light, rather than a colour). Because of this blackness, the light detectors there sent comparatively few messages back to your brain. The rod detectors in particular actually become slightly more sensitive to light (or dark adapted) because they were trying to detect as much light as they could. However, the bright whitish area on the paper surrounding the black ghost also formed on your retina and these light detecting cells had to work hard to send the messages to your brain (because white light contains a lot of light). In fact some of the rod detectors here became slightly less sensitive to light (or light adapted) because they were working so hard. So by the time you switched your stare into the bright whiteness of the graveyard scene, the area of your retina sending this bright whitish information back to your brain had become rather tired and less sensitive, and so did not respond very well to the whiteness of the graveyard scene. This made much of the scene actually appear slightly darker, being light grey rather than white, though you probably didn't notice this. The area of your retina where the black ghost had formed had done comparatively very little work while staring at the ghost and had become slightly more sensitive to light. So as soon as you switched your stare to the bright graveyard scene, this ghost-shape area of light detectors now suddenly got bright whitish light shining from the paper and, partly because they had become slightly more sensitive, sent a lot of information about the white surface back to your brain. So, for the same graveyard scene, the more central ghost-shape area of more sensitive cells on your retina were sending more information to the brain than the surrounding more tired or less sensitive cells. The net result is that you saw a negative after-image in the form of a bright whitish ghostly figure floating within the less bright (or grey) graveyard scene. So the ghost actually appeared to be whiter than white paper!

WHERE ON EARTH?

The negative after-image effect you get in this experiment, particularly the grey darkening you see around your glowing ghostly after-image, is the same as that experienced by anybody who has ever had a photograph taken by someone using a flash on their camera. If you've had your picture taken using a flash, you may remember that everything looks a little darker for a few seconds after you'd seen the flash. You may also remember seeing the annoying little dark blob that stays in view wherever you look- this is from the very bright light from the window of the flash gun itself and will probably look the same shape.

SOME TRICK TIPS!

- ...**It's OK to blink-** just try to close and open your eyes as quickly as you can each time you blink.
- ...**Ghost picture-** getting fuzzy and darker while you stare is OK-it means you're staring properly.
- ...**Stare longer-** if you don't easily see the ghostly after-image, try staring at the black ghost for longer.
- ...**Blinking brings the image back-** the after-image won't last very long, but blinking every second or two while looking at the graveyard scene will usually make it last the longest.
- ...**Rest your eyes for a minute or two-** it takes about this long for your eyes to go back to normal.

ANSWERS TO SOME OF THE NUMBERED QUESTIONS:

ANS. 2: Staring at different coloured ghost pictures will produce different coloured negative after-images. The thing about negative after-images is that the after-image is always the opposite or complimentary colour of the picture you initially stared at. For example, you discovered at the start of this experiment that staring at an almost blackish picture produces a whitish ghostly after-image. So we can say that white and black are complimentary shades. You will discover that red ghosts produce green /bluish after-images, yellow ghosts produce bluish after-images, green ghosts produce pinkish after-images, and blue ghosts produce yellowish afterimages. I've used 'ish' at the end of each after-image colour because what colour you actually see depends on a number of things including the shade and brightness of the colour you use for the ghost picture and how bright the shining light is.

The reason that you see different colour after-images is to do with the tiring out of the colour light detection cells (or cones) on the retina. To allow you to see in colour there are three different types of cone cells sensitive to red, green and blue light. If you mix red, blue and green light together in the correct amounts, then you can create any other colour, including white. White light stimulates all three different cone cells equally and so they all tire equally. However, light of any other colour will tire some colour cones more than others. For example, red light, tires the red cones the most. The longer you stare at something red, the fewer and fewer signals get sent to your brain from the red cones. If you then quickly change your stare to a blank white space, the red cones are too tired to send enough signal to your brain, but the blue and green cones are working OK. So instead of getting the same amount of signal from each colour cone to see white, your brain receives more signals from the green and blue cones and so you see a green/bluish after-image.

ANS. 3: Some other things you could change and explore include:
- ...Using different coloured bright light sources;
- ...Using brighter or less bright light sources;
- ...Using ghost pictures of different colour tones, such as light grey & dark grey, or light blue & dark blue;
- ...Staring at the ghosts picture for different lengths of time;
- ...Holding the book at different distances from your eyes, both when staring at the ghost picture and/or when staring into the graveyard scene;
- ...Copying your coloured ghost picture and/or graveyard scene onto different colour sheets of paper
- ...Staring at your ghost picture and then somewhere into the room or at a blank wall;
- ...Timing for how long you can see the ghostly after-image for different experiments.

© Dr Mark Biddiss 2001, 2005, 2011, Magical Science Book 1 @ www.Dr-Mark.co.uk

19 SOAPY SPEED BOATS, PETRIFIED PEPPER & WATER RINGS

OBJECTIVE: To have fun exploring some of the strange properties of water's stretchy skin in four simple experiments.

WHAT YOU NEED: Washing up liquid (or other liquid detergent), a bowel or sink of water (make sure that whatever container you use is very clean with no traces of soap or detergent anywhere otherwise the experiments won't work), a pencil, a small piece of cardboard, a pair of scissors, a length of very thin sewing thread (about as long as your hand) tied into a small loop, some finely ground pepper and a sewing needle.

SOME OF THE SCIENCE YOU'RE EXPLORING: Chemistry: Properties of materials: liquids, bonding, water, surface tension, Physics: Physical Processes, forces & motion, Biology: Life Processes & Living Things: movement.

1 Cut your small piece of cardboard into a boat-shape. Start with a rectangle-shape piece of card about 5 or 6cm long and about 2 or 3cm wide. Cut it to be pointed at one end for the front of the boat (the bow) and along the back edge (the stern) cut out a small triangle-shaped hole. If you don't cut the triangle of card out completely, you can bend it upwards and use it as a handle.

2 Gripping the triangle-shaped handle, VERY GENTLY rest your boat on the surface of the water in your bowl or sink.

3 Dip the pointed end of your pencil in some washing-up liquid and then hold the pencil-point just over the triangle-shaped hole in the stern of your boat. Wait for a drop of washing-up liquid to fall into the gap or quickly and gently touch the surface of the water within the triangle-shape hole.

© Dr Mark Biddiss 2001, 2005, 2011, Magical Science Book 1 @ www.Dr-Mark.co.uk

WHAT HAPPENS?

Instantly your cardboard boat will shoot across the surface of the water like a speed-boat!

SOME QUESTIONS TO THINK ABOUT

1. What do you think is going on? (see 'SO WHAT'S GOING ON?')
2. What happens when you add more washing-up liquid to the boat once it has stopped?
3. What happens if you start again with a clean bowl of water, but instead of using a boat, this time sprinkle just a small amount of finely ground pepper all over the surface of the water and drip your washing-up liquid into the centre of the water's surface? (answer provided)
4. What happens if you start over yet again, but instead of using a boat or pepper, you float a small loop of very thin sewing thread on the surface of the water and drip your washing-up liquid into the inside of the loop? (answer provided)
5. What other things (variables) could you change to explore what happens? (some suggestions provided)

(Numbered answers and explanations to some of the questions are given on the next page)

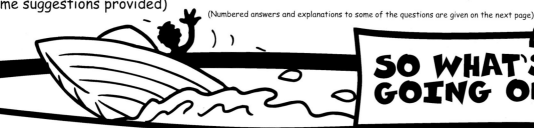

SO WHAT'S GOING ON?

Your boat is resting on what can be thought of as the thin, stretchy skin layer of the water. Water particles or molecules pull on each other to stick together. Water molecules at the surface (between water and air) have no water molecules to pull against on the air side. So to make up for this they pull more strongly against the other molecules next to them. This helps to form a strong surface layer that behaves like a stretchy skin and is called the meniscus. The pull from the water molecules that forms this stretchy meniscus skin is called surface tension, and is pretty much the same strength in all directions across the surface of the water.

Now, when you add washing-up liquid (or any other kind of soap or detergent) to water, the washing-up liquid molecules mix with the water molecules and pull to stick to them. Water molecules are attracted to stick to washing-up liquid molecules more than they are to each other. This loosening or weakening of the attraction of each water molecule to each other means that they become less sticky and so spread further apart. This effectively weakens the meniscus skin of the water in that area, making it thinner and even stretchier.

OK: lets get back to the boat. When you gently rested your boat on the meniscus skin of the water, the surface tension of the water molecules pulled it equally in all directios; that's why it could rest without moving. However, when you dripped some washing-up liquid into the water at the back end of the boat, the washing-up liquid weakened the surface tension or pull of the meniscus skin in that area. So this weakened the pull of the meniscus on the back end of the boat. Because the surface tension of the meniscus at the opposite end of the boat (the front) had not yet weakened and so was now stronger, the boat was pulled swiftly in that direction.

WHERE ON EARTH?

Water's stretchy meniscus skin is strong enough to hold up some water insects, such as pond skaters or surface striders. These insect's bodies are actually heavier and denser than water, and so should sink. Not only don't they sink, these insects can actually stand, walk and skate across the surface of the meniscus skin! Special hairs on their bodies and long legs allow them to spread their weight more evenly and barely even dent the meniscus skin's surface. This prevents them from breaking through.

Using the same trick as the water insects, you can even rest a sewing needle on the meniscus skin of water without it falling through and sinking! (One way is to carefully place a lightly greased but otherwise dry needle on a small piece of paper tissue. Gently float the tissue and needle on the surface of some clean water. With the prongs of two forks, VERY gently push the tissue down at each end to sink it into the water. This should leave your needle resting on the surface!).

SOME TRICK TIPS!

- ...REMEMBER: **Use a clean bowl or sink** - before you start each new experiment the bowl or sink must be clean of any soap, washing-up liquid or any other detergent, otherwise the experiment will not work.

- ...**Smooth, still & shallow**- you don't need deep water. A centimetre or so in the bottom of a flat-bottomed bowl or sink will do fine. Also make sure that the surface of your water is smooth and still before you start.

ANSWERS TO SOME OF THE NUMBERED QUESTIONS:

ANS. 3: The pepper quickly shoots outwards in all directions towards the sides of the bowl and away from the centre where you dripped the washing-up liquid. Some of the pepper will sink too. It's as if the pepper was scared and petrified of the washing-up liquid! Actually, each piece of pepper is part of the same tug-of-war going on in the meniscus skin of the water, as was going on in your boat experiment. Before adding the washing-up liquid, the water molecules of the meniscus (supporting and surrounding each speck of pepper) pulled on each other with equal surface tension in all directions across the surface of the water. Just as with your boat experiment above, adding washing-up liquid weakened the pull, or surface tension, of the water molecules in that area, causing them to spread apart. However, the surface tension of the meniscus surrounding and away from the washing-up liquid still pulled in all directions just as strongly. So, the weaker meniscus in the centre allowed the surrounding stronger pulling meniscus to pull it outwards in all directions towards the sides of the bowl, dragging the pepper along for the ride! The pepper that sinks is actually denser than water and only stays up in the first place because of the strength of the meniscus at the start.

ANS. 4: The uneven cotton loop will suddenly form into an almost perfect circle. As with your boat and pepper experiments, the surface tension of the meniscus was pulling on all sides of the thread equally, both inside and outside the loop. When you dripped washing-up liquid inside the loop, the surface tension of the enclosed meniscus became weaker. However, outside and surrounding the loop, the surface tension of the meniscus there was still just as strong and carried on pulling on the thread equally in all directions. The weaker meniscus pulling inwards within the loop was no match for the stronger meniscus pulling outwards on the outside of the loop. The loop formed a circle because the outside meniscus pulled outwards equally in all directions towards the sides of the bowl.

ANS. 5: Other things you could change and explore include:
- ...Drip a bigger or smaller drop of washing-up liquid into the triangle-shape hole in the boat;
- ...Use a weaker washing-up liquid (or detergent), or just water down the one you already used;
- ...Cut the boat from thicker or thinner card or other sheet materials;
- ...Cut different shape boats and different size boats;
- ...Cut different shaped holes in the back of the boat;
- ...Cut the hole in different positions along the back edge of the boat or even along the sides;
- ...Try hotter and colder water;
- ...Try other brands of washing-up liquid or liquid detergents.

(20) FLYING FLIPPING FISH

OBJECTIVE:
To have fun exploring spinning flight using a paper strip model and how changes in the design affect the way the model spins and glides down to the ground.

SOME OF THE SCIENCE YOU'RE EXPLORING:
Physics: Physical Processes: flight, forces & motion, pressure, friction, air-resistance, Chemistry: Properties of Materials, air, Biology: Life Processes & Living things, movement, flying things.

WHAT YOU NEED:
Some paper, a ruler, some scissors and a pencil or pen.

1 Cut a strip of paper somewhere between 20 to 30cm long and 2 to 3cm wide. Note your measurements.

2 Make a cut exactly halfway across the width of the strip, about 3 or 4cm from one end. Turn the strip around and do the same thing the other end. Make sure that your two cuts come from opposite sides of the strip towards the centre, one cut from one long edge and one from the opposite long edge.

3 Bend the strip in the middle, bring the two ends together and form a closed loop by sliding the cut slot at one end into the slot at the other end. You should end up with something that looks like a round-nosed fish.

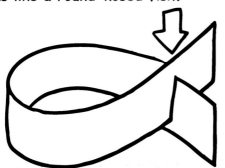

4 Grip the paper fish by one side (not by the nose or tail) and hold it so that the fish looks like its swimming on its side and towards your right. Then lift it high above your head in this swimming position and drop it.

© Dr Mark Biddiss 2001, 2005, 2011, Magical Science Book 1 @ www.Dr-Mark.co.uk

WHAT HAPPENS?

The fish should spin its way down to the ground, gliding not quite straight down but in a steeply sloping and slightly spiralling path, and probably towards you!

SOME QUESTIONS TO THINK ABOUT

1. What do you think is going on? (see 'SO WHAT'S GOING ON?')

2. How can you make the fish fall in a steeply sloping and slightly spiralling path but in the opposite direction? (answer provided)

3. How does the fish glide down if you fold and crease the nose of the fish to make it pointed rather than rounded? (answer provided)

4. How does the fish spin and fall if you make cuts at different distances from the end of the strip so as to alter the length of the tail pieces, making them longer, shorter, or each of a different length?

5. What other things (variables) could you change to explore what happens? (some suggestions provided)

(Numbered answers and explanations to some of the questions are given on the next page)

SO WHAT'S GOING ON?

As soon as you release the fish, the pull of gravity causes it to fall. As the fish falls it is pulled down through the air that's in the way. Because the air rubs against the falling fish, it acts like a rubbing brake and slows down the fall of the fish. We call this braking or slowing action air-friction or more commonly air-resistance. When you let go of the fish, one side will drop slightly lower than the other. Frequently, when you simply let go of the fish, the side you're not gripping, and so which is furthest away from you, drops lower first. This starts the fish spinning, with the bottom surface coming towards you and the top surface moving away from you. If you hold your fish with the nose pointing to the right, simply letting go usually causes the fish to spin clockwise if you were looking at it from the front. The fish carried on spinning because gravity keeps on pulling it down and the air rubs past and pushes against some parts of the fish slightly differently to other parts. Because the spin of the fish happens by itself without your help, we can call it autorotation. The fish spins in a sloping and spiralling path because of its shape and as it spins, it creates a small amount of lift underneath which helps to hold it up in the air.

WHERE ON EARTH?

Some plant and tree seeds autorotate or spin as they fly through the air and fall to the ground. A good example of this will be the seeds from Ash trees, as well as those from Maple and Sycamore trees. The seeds from these trees are sometimes known as helicopter seeds (though helicopters won't grow from them!). In fact, you may notice that the way your fish spins when it has very long tail pieces is very similar to the way the seeds of these trees fall. Now, if you drop your spinning fish in a light breeze outdoors, you'll probably notice that the breeze can carry it further and make it take even longer to get to the ground. This is what happens with the spinning seeds from these trees. When the seed drops from the tree and starts spinning, any breeze will help to carry it so that it lands further from the tree than it would have had it just fallen straight to the ground without spinning. Being further from the parent tree may give the seed a better chance of growing into a tree itself (partly because it won't be in the shade of the parent tree or have to share its water and soil nutrients), and so continue the rich tapestry of life!.

SOME TRICK TIPS!

...**Avoid drafts-** do your experiments indoors at first to avoid any air breeze or draughts, as these will affect how your fish spins and falls. You could always repeat the experiment outside in a breeze or draft later on to look for any difference.

...**Stand on a chair-** this will make it easier to see how the fish spins and falls, because they'll have further to fall. **JUST DO BE VERY CAREFUL NOT TO FALL!**

...**Keep a record of your cuts-** when cutting your strips and slots, keep a record of the measurements of the size of the strip and where you made the cuts. This will make it easier to plan what changes you want to try.

ANSWERS TO SOME OF THE NUMBERED QUESTIONS:

ANS. 2: Causing the fish to spin in the opposite direction to which it did the first time will cause it to fall to the ground in the opposite direction. You should discover that a clockwise spin (looking at the nose of the fish) causes the fish to fall to the ground in a sloping path to the fish's right (or towards you if you drop the fish while it points to your right). You may also notice that the fish will fall in a slight spiral in a clockwise direction (as viewed from above). The fish falls and spirals in the opposite directions if you cause it to spin counter or anticlockwise. (If holding the fish up in the air and with its nose pointing to the right, you can cause it to spin counter or anticlockwise by giving it a VERY GENTLE flick with your wrist, upwards and away from you. This will cause the fish to fall away from you rather than towards you and it will fall in a slightly counter or anti-clockwise spiralling path.)

ANS. 3: Giving your fish a pointed nose will cause it to spin faster and take longer to get to the ground, and along a slightly less steep path than before. The faster spin as it falls down the spiralling path gives the fish a little more lift from the air from underneath and so keeps it in the air for a little longer.

ANS. 5: Other things you could change and explore include:

...Making the paper strip longer or shorter;

...Making the paper strip wider or narrower;

...Cut out shapes along the body of the fish and its tail;

...Add paperclips or wrap sticky tape around different parts of the fish to alter its shape and weight in these places;

...Make your fish from different kinds of paper and other sheet materials, such as metal baking foil or plastic.

...Make more cuts further from the ends of the strip so as to make a fish with two or more loops in its body.

© Dr Mark Biddiss 2001, 2005, 2011, Magical Science Book 1 @ www.Dr-Mark.co.uk

21 COLOUR-NAMES & NAMING-COLOURS

WHAT YOU NEED:
One or two sheets of white paper (you'll be writing words so lined paper might be better for you), a selection of different colour bright marker pens or crayons (have at least four different colours if you can and only use yellow if it's easy to read). You also need a grown-up and perhaps a very young child just able to read and make sure nobody is colour-blind!).

OBJECTIVE:
To have fun exploring some of the ways we read words and see colours, and what happens when we try to mix the two together!

SOME OF THE SCIENCE YOU'RE EXPLORING:
Biology: Life Processes & Living Things: Ourselves, senses, vision & seeing.

1 Using your colour pens, you need to copy out the following two lists of words (best in capital letters) into two columns onto a sheet of white paper. Use a different colour to write each word. To make things more interesting, I suggest that you use your black, blue and brown marker pens to write the words BLACK, BLUE and BROWN. But it's important to make sure that you DON'T write any of the colour names with a marker pen of that same colour. For example, don't write the word BLUE with the blue marker, or the word RED with the red marker. Also, DON'T use the same colour marker pen to write words that are next to each other, one above the other. I suggest leaving a gap of at least two or three words before you use the same colour marker again to write another word. So, here's your two lists of words to copy out:

BUS	RED
MUM	GREEN
TABLE	BLUE
CAT	YELLOW
GIRL	BLACK
BALL	BROWN
CAR	YELLOW
DOOR	BLUE
TOY	RED
DAD	BROWN
HOUSE	BLACK
BOY	GREEN

2 Read both lists of words out loud as quickly as you reasonably can (certainly don't take longer than you need);

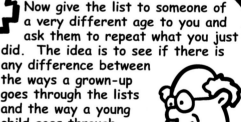

3 Now go through the lists again but this time DON'T read the words. Instead look at each word and say out loud what colour it's written in. Again, go through the list as quickly as you can.

4 Now give the list to someone of a very different age to you and ask them to repeat what you just did. The idea is to see if there is any difference between the ways a grown-up goes through the lists and the way a young child goes through the lists.

WHAT HAPPENS?

It usually takes a very young child about the same time to read what the words say in both columns, as it does for them to go through and name the colours used to write each word. However, most older children and adults take a lot longer to go through and name the colours used than to simply read the words themselves. And they'll probably take the longest to list the colours used to write the colour names in the right-hand column.

SOME QUESTIONS TO THINK ABOUT?

1. What do you think is going on? (see 'SO WHAT'S GOING ON?')

2. Why did I suggest that it may be more interesting if you used black, blue and brown marker pens to write the words BLACK, BLUE and BROWN? (answer provided)

3. Why do you think older children and adults take even longer to say the colours used in the right-hand column? (answer provided)

4. How quickly do older children and adults name the colours used in the two columns if they turn the sheet of paper around so that the words are upside-down? (answer provided)

5. How quickly do you think you could name the colours used in the two columns if you were to look at the words through blurred vision so as to make the words less clear and difficult to read? Perhaps you could look at the words with your eyelids almost closed or remove any spectacles if you wear them. (answer provided)

6. Do you think grown-ups who are artists or use colour a lot in their work would have the same problems naming the colours used to write the words? (answer provided)

(Numbered answers and explanations to some of the questions are given on the next page)

SO WHAT'S GOING ON?

So just why does it take most older children and grown-ups longer to name the colours used than to read what the words say? Well, it's simply that older people are more used to reading words when they see them and not saying what colour they're written in. What the word actually says is usually more important to them.

When you ask most readers to name the colour a word is written in, probably the first thing their brain actually does is read what the word says, because that's usually the most important thing they need to know. Another part of their brain sees and recognises the colour the word is written in. But because they are so used to reading a word when they see it rather than saying what colour it's written in, their poor old brain ends up getting a bit confused! The confusion arises because you're asking them something about the word that isn't usually so important to them. All this brain confusion wastes time and slows them down. So much for multi-tasking brains!

© Dr Mark Biddiss 2001, 2005, 2011, Magical Science Book 1 @ www.Dr-Mark.co.uk

WHERE ON EARTH?

Artists and graphic designers who use colour should be especially careful not to confuse their readers when using colour to write any of the colour names in their written work. This is particularly important on places where the writing may often be read very quickly by the reader, such as on the covers of books, magazines, roadside display posters or even paint tins. After all, you'd be pretty annoyed if you journeyed miles to somewhere to buy a tin of beautiful blue paint only to arrive home and open the tin to find that you'd actually bought brown paint instead! (But did they write the colour name BROWN in blue, or the name BLUE in brown?).

SOME TRICK TIPS!

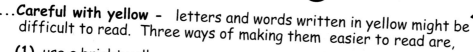

...**Careful with yellow** - letters and words written in yellow might be difficult to read. Three ways of making them easier to read are,

(1) use a bright yellow,

(2) draw your letters using thick lines,

(3) draw around the edges or outline the thick yellow lines with a very thin black or dark line, so it looks like each letter is hollow and has been coloured-in with yellow.

ANSWERS TO SOME OF THE NUMBERED QUESTIONS:

ANS. 2: If you think about it, the colour names black, blue and brown all start with the same letter and so all start with the same 'b' sound. So if you write the word BLACK with a blue marker pen, your reader is more likely to take even longer to correctly name the colour used to write it because it has the same sound for the start of both words. Wicked aren't I!

ANS. 3: Some readers take even longer to say the colours used to write the words in the right-hand column because the words themselves are the names of colours. So the adult's poor brain is even more confused than when it was just looking at the colours of words that were not the names of colours, as listed in the first column. So if you write the colour name BROWN using a blue marker pen, part of your brain thinks, "It says BROWN", while another part says, "Yes, but it looks blue!;" and confusion sets in!

ANS. 4: Many readers can name the colours used more quickly if the page is turned upside-down. Most don't even try to read the upside-down words and so their brain finds it easier and quicker to name the colours used. Mind you, it doesn't always work very well on grown-ups who read and write a lot in their jobs because these people's brains are much better at recognizing words when looked at from different angles and directions, even upside-down!

ANS. 5: If your reader can find some way of blurring their vision and looking at the words so that the words appear unclear and difficult to read, they are likely to be quicker in naming the colours used. If the words are un-readable, your reader's brain will simply find it quicker to name the colours because it has not been confused with what the words say as well.

ANS. 6: From my few investigations I've found that for grown-ups who use colour a lot, the difference between the time it takes them to read the columns of words and the time it takes them to then name the colours used is noticeably LESS than the difference in time taken for the two activities by grown-ups who don't use colour so much. Put another way, if an artist and an adult who is not an artist take the same length of time to read the words in the columns, the artist will probably be quicker at naming the colours used.

22. CRUSHING CANS & SHRINKING BOTTLES

OBJECTIVE: To have fun exploring how to crush metal cans and plastic bottles with hot & cold air, and hot & cold water.

WANTED GROWN-UP HELP

WHAT YOU NEED:
A baking tray or bowl full of chilled or ice-cold water, a tablespoon, a little more water (preferably hot), one or more empty ring-pull aluminium soft drink cans, a cooking stove burner or hot-plate (adult help wanted especially here), some heat-proof tongs or a good oven mitt with thumb to securely hold the can (you could make some tongs out of a wire clothes hanger). For the safer and easier similar experiment you'll need a plastic drinks bottle with screw-on cap and a hair blow-dryer.

SOME OF THE SCIENCE YOU'RE EXPLORING:
Physics: Physical Processes: forces & pressure, unbalanced forces,
Chemistry: Properties of Materials: solids, liquids & gases, boiling, evaporation and condensation.

1 Place your tray or bowl of chilled water on a work surface as near as you can to your cooking stove;

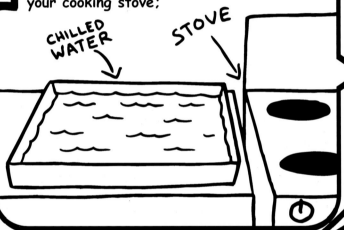
CHILLED WATER — STOVE

2 Then add a tablespoon or so of water (preferably hot) to an empty ring-pull aluminium soft-drink can, just enough to cover the bottom inside. Using hot water will help speed things up a little.

3 With an adult's help, heat the can (with water inside) on the stove burner or hotplate until the water boils. When you see plenty of so-called steam coming from the can, let the water boil vigorously for one more minute. (By the way, what most people call steam is really condensed water vapour, steam is actually invisible. Also, NEVER EVER HEAT A SEALED OR CLOSED METAL CAN.)

4 After one minute, grip the can near the bottom carefully and securely with the tongs or oven mitt, as near to the heat as possible. Now brace yourself, and in one swift movement, quickly lift the can off the stove, turn the can over and place it upside-down in the chilled water in the tray or bowl. You must be swift with this last step, maybe practice it a few times first before you do the real experiment.

AND DONT FORGET TO TURN THE STOVE OFF AT THE END EITHER!

© Dr Mark Biddiss 2001, 2005, 2011, Magical Science Book 1 @ www.Dr-Mark.co.uk

The upside down can is crushed and collapses almost immediately after it goes into the chilled water. In fact, it happens so fast that it'll probably make you jump! Now you see why I said 'Now brace yourself!'

SOME QUESTIONS TO THINK ABOUT

1. What do you think is going on? (see 'SO WHAT'S GOING ON?')
2. What other things (variables) could you change to explore what happens? (some suggestions provided)
3. How could you do a much safer and easier similar experiment using just a plastic drinks bottle with its screw-on cap and a hair blow-dryer? (suggestion provided)

(Numbered answers and explanations to the questions are given on the next page)

SO WHAT'S GOING ON?

Believe it or not, the can is crushed by the air-pressure outside surrounding it! Just before you heat the water, the can is filled mostly with air plus a little water. When you heat the water hot enough, it boils and vaporises or evaporates, turning from hot liquid water into hot water vapour or steam. As soon as the hot water vapour leaves the water it starts to cool. This causes it to condense, turning from a hot invisible gas into thousands of tiny droplets of water that together appear as a white, smoky mist or cloud. The water vapour pushes the air out of the can, along with some other water vapour as well. This leaves the can almost entirely filled with water vapour plus a little boiling water in the bottom. Now, because the water vapour particles or molecules are so hot, they have lots of energy, and so are very fast moving. So fast and with so much energy, in fact, that the water vapour molecules inside the can collide against the inside walls of the can with about the same push or pressure as the air molecules pressing against the can from the outside. Put another way, the water vapour pressure inside the can is at this time the same as the air pressure outside the can and so the can stays intact.

However, all this changes when you turn the can upside-down into the chilled water. When this happens, the chilled water very quickly helps cool the hot water vapour inside the can. When the water vapour molecules cool they lose energy, which causes them to slow down and get closer together, taking up less space. Slower moving molecules don't push so hard against the inside walls of the can either. Very quickly the hot water vapour cools down enough and condenses, turning from a gas or vapour back into liquid again. The molecules in liquid water are much, much closer together than molecules in water vapour, and so take up much, much less space. In fact, a can full of hot water vapour cools to produce only a drop of liquid water. This water and small amount of cooler water vapour left doesn't push outwards very much on the inside walls of the can. With very little pressure inside the can pushing outwards, the air pressure outside the can pushing inwards is now much, much stronger. The aluminium metal of the can is not strong enough to resist and so is crushed rapidly in what can be called an implosion! A little chilled water from your bowl is pushed into the can by the greater air pressure outside while all this is going on, but the air crushes the can too quickly before much water can enter.

WHERE ON EARTH?

As your experiments demonstrate, a sealed or closed container can collapse or implode when the pressure outside is much stronger than the pressure inside. This is something submarine designers need to know about. Submarines or subs may need to be able to dive very deep underwater. The deeper they dive, the more the water pushes in against them from outside. The air pressure on the inside, however, has to be kept about the same all the time for the people inside. So the deeper the sub dives, the bigger the difference between the water pressure outside and the air pressure inside. That means the deeper a sub needs to go, the stronger the skin or hull needs to be to resist the water pressure outside. About three-quarters of the Earth's oceans are somewhere between 3 and 6 kilometres deep. In a few places they go as deep as 11 kilometres! Although one or two amazingly strong subs have been made to go to the bottom of the deepest oceans, most subs would be at risk of collapsing or imploding if they went no more than even 1 kilometre deep. In practice, when subs have gone too deep because of an accident, rather than suddenly implode, what normally happens is that water pushes its way into the sub through a small fracture or crack that forms in the hull, and fills the sub with water.

SOME TRICK TIPS!

...Make sure the can is light-weight aluminium- steel cans may be too strong to collapse very easily.

...Grip the can with the tongs or oven mitt with your palm facing upwards- this will make it much easier for you to lift the can and swiftly turn it over upside-down and place it in the chilled water.

ANSWERS TO SOME OF THE NUMBERED QUESTIONS:

ANS. 2: Other things you could change and explore include:

...Try using warmer or even colder water in the bowl or tray;

...Wait a few seconds after taking the steaming can from the heat before putting it in the water;

...Try putting the can the right-side up in the chilled water;

...Try the same experiment but with an empty can instead of one with a little hot water in it;

...Try different size cans;

...Try the same size cans with different size holes;

...Try steel cans.

ANS. 3: One way of doing a similar, though much safer and easier, version of this experiment using a plastic drinks bottle and hair blow-dryer is as follows:

1. Screw the cap onto the empty plastic bottle, but only screw it on very loosely at this point you should be able to easily squeeze the bottle to force air out through the loosely fitted cap;

2. For at least 30 seconds, heat the bottle all over using the hair blow-dryer on its hottest setting;

3. After the 30 seconds, quickly screw the cap on very tightly and wait patiently to see what happens.

After a short time - and quite suddenly - the bottle will start to collapse. The explanation is very similar to your **CRUSHING CAN** experiment. In brief, as you warmed up the air in the bottle you gave the air molecules more energy. This caused them to move around faster and further apart from each other, which caused the air in the bottle as a whole to expand. Because the air expanded, its pressure increased and forced some air out of the bottle through the loosely fitted cap. When you screwed the cap up tightly and stopped heating the bottle, the air molecules inside started to cool down again and so lose energy. As they lost energy they slowed down and moved closer to each other again. But because some air molecules had been pushed out, there was now fewer left in the bottle than when you started. Fewer molecules take up less space and so don't push so hard against the inside wall of the bottle. So the air pressure outside was greater than that inside and the bottle collapsed or imploded just like the can. Other things you could try with this bottle experiment include: use different size and shape bottles; bottles made of thicker or thinner plastic; heat the bottle for more or less time; and cool the bottle more quickly in the refrigerator or freezer.

23. UNREADABLE WORDS & INVISIBLE LETTERS

OBJECTIVE: To have fun exploring some of the ways we may not be able to see and read words and letters.

Watch out for deliberate mistakes!

WHAT YOU NEED: This book, some writing paper, a pen or pencil, a ruler, a grown-up and a child (one of these may be you).

SOME OF THE SCIENCE YOU'RE EXPLORING: Biology: Life Processes & Living Things: Ourselves, senses, vision and perception, & word perception.

1. As quickly as you can read out loud the phrases in the two triangles below.

Triangle 1: I LOVE PARIS IN THE THE SPRINGTIME

Triangle 2: A BIRD IN THE THE HAND

2. Read them both through out loud again, but this time look at the words more closely and read more slowly.

3. Now go through the sentence below quickly and just once, and count how many times the letter F appears:

FINISHED FILES ARE THE RE-
SULT OF YEARS OF SCIENTIF-
IC STUDY COMBINED WITH THE
EXPERIENCE OF MANY YEARS

4. Now give the book to someone of a very different age to you and ask them to repeat what you just did.

78 © Dr Mark Biddiss 2001, 2005, 2011, Magical Science Book 1 @ www.Dr-Mark.co.uk

WHAT HAPPENS?

On first reading the phrases in the triangles, most people read, I LOVE PARIS IN THE SPRINGTIME, and, A BIRD IN THE HAND. The phrases should actually read, I LOVE PARIS IN THE THE SPRINGTIME, and, A BIRD IN THE THE HAND (I hope you didn't miss any words again this time!). Most people see only the second THE in each phrase, especially if they read as fast as they can. Grown-ups are more likely to miss the second THE than young children, especially those children who are only just learning or beginning to read.

With the F-counting experiment, on the first counting, most people see only three, and sometimes four of the letter F's. There are actually six! How many did you see I wonder? I bet if you only saw three then you probably missed the three in the words OF. Am I right? And just as with the phrases in the triangles, grown-ups are more likely to make mistakes than young children are.

SOME QUESTIONS TO THINK ABOUT

1. What do you think is going on? (see 'SO WHAT'S GOING ON?')

2. What happens if you repeat the first part of the experiment but this time copy and re-write the words inside the triangles, leaving the two THEs in exactly the same position but swap all the other words around to make a nonsense phrase? (answer provided)

3. The way people usually pronounce the letter F is also thought to affect how many they count in the F counting experiment. Can you suggest why this may be so? (answer provided)

4. Why do you think that people who have difficulty with their reading or less experienced readers (such as young children) are not so easily fooled in any of these experiments? (answer provided)

5. Is there any difference to the results of either experiment if you write the sentences along one single line?

6. Can you write sentences of your own which catch people out with the number of THEs and Fs?

(Numbered answers and explanations to some of the questions are given on the next page)

SO WHAT'S GOING ON?

With experienced readers, they often don't give as much attention or importance to the short and familiar words in a sentence as they do to the longer and less familiar words. This is particularly so with those short words which function as definite or indefinite articles (such as the words, the, a, an, and some) or conjunctions (such as the words, and, but and if). These short words are even more likely to go unnoticed if they are placed at the end of a line (as in our phrases in the triangles). Also, an experienced reader becomes very familiar with the shape of many of these short, common words. These shapes are memorised and the reader may no longer even see the words as being necessarily made up of separate letters and sounds, or even as being made up of letters at all! This is one reason why the letter F is not seen in the words OF in the F-counting experiment.

© Dr Mark Biddiss 2001, 2005, 2011, Magical Science Book 1 @ www.Dr-Mark.co.uk

WHERE ON EARTH?

Proof-readers are people who read through the text for books and other pieces of writing to make sure that they are written correctly in spelling and grammar, before they finally get printed and published. These people have to be especially on the look out for short repeat words such as THE THE, as written in the phrases in the triangles. To make their job a bit easier, many computer word processors warn of these repeated word mistakes very easily. Even my computer spotted the the second THE in the the second to last sentence! Also, if a proof-reader was asked to have a go at the F-counting experiment, they would very likely count all six first time. This is because they are aware of this reading problem and have learnt to see and read words in a slightly different way to most people, paying closer attention and seeing all words as being important.

SOME TRICK TIPS!

...**Test different people away from each other** - if you want to get other people to do these experiments, you get better results if you don't let them hear what other people read and say before it's their turn.

ANSWERS TO SOME OF THE NUMBERED QUESTIONS:

ANS. 2: People are more likely to see both THEs if all the other words in the triangle have been swapped around to make a nonsense phrase with no meaning. With the first experiment, one of the reasons why the first THE in each of the phrases is often not read is because it doesn't fit in with what we would expect to see in such a familar and sensible sounding phrase. The familiarity of these two phrases to many grown-ups in particular just adds to the difficulty some of them may have in reading the sentence correctly and noticing that the word THE actually appears twice. In other words, most experienced readers such as grown-ups tend to read what they expect to see, particularly when reading at their normal speed. Interestingly, scientists would say that a subconscious part of your brain (a part of your brain that you're not aware of) does actually see both of the words THE. But because it wouldn't make sense in the phrase, that subconscious part of your brain decides not to tell the other conscious part of your brain (the conscious part of your brain being the one you are aware of and usually think to yourself with). Interesting idea!

ANS. 3: When most people read they think of particular sounds with particular letters. This is called phonetic reading. When you are scanning through the sentence looking for the letter F, scientists reckon that part of your brain is actually reading each word and looking for the letter with the F-sound. So, one of the reasons why many people miss the letter F in the word OF is because the F in this word is actually pronounced with a V-sound rather than an F-sound. In the words, FINISHED, FILES, and SCIENTIFIC, the F has its usual F-sound, as with F in the word FLOWER.

But if all this stuff about F-sounds (and missing short words) is true, why do some people notice the F in the last OF and miss the other two? Well, this may be because this last OF is positioned near to the end of the sentence where your eyes would have come to a stop when you'd finished scanning. The fact that your eyes had stopped very nearby would have made that F easier to actually see.

ANS. 4: People who have difficulty with their reading or less experienced readers are less likely to be fooled and so more likely to see all the words and letters they are reading for, because they simply look more carefully at all the words. To them, as with our proof-reader, all the words are seen as important and so they give them all the same attention. Inexperienced readers usually read much slower as well and this also helps. As you now know, as we learn to read faster, we give more attention to longer and unfamiliar words, which seem more important, and skip the shorter apparently less important words. And the faster we read, the more short words we skip, and so we are more likely to make the sort of mistakes you investigated in these experiments.

24. VANISHING RINGS & LINKING LOOPS

OBJECTIVE: To have fun exploring the making and cutting of twisted and one-sided loops around the middle to find still only one loop or two loops linked together like chain-links, or knotted loops.

SOME OF THE SCIENCE YOU'RE EXPLORING:
Mathematics: Topology (deforming surfaces);
Physics: Physical Processes: transferring energy (belt drives).

WHAT YOU NEED:
Several strips of paper about 30cm long (any longer is OK) and about 3cm wide, a pair of round-nosed safety scissors, some sticky-tape and a pencil or pen (optional).

1
Take a strip of paper and bend it around to make a loop or band, overlapping the ends of the strip by about 1cm.

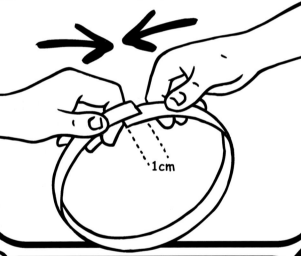

2
Take hold of one of the overlapping ends, twist or turn it over half a turn (through 180 degrees) and then place it back overlapping the other end again. Then use sticky tape to stick the overlapping ends together. You should now have a loop or band with a half-twist in it.

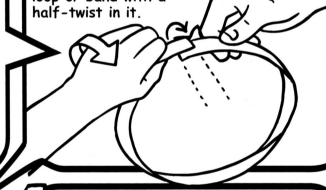

3
Using the scissors, CAREFULLY cut the loop length-ways along the centre of the strip, as if trying to cut it into two separate thinner loops. Cut right the way around the loop and see what happens.

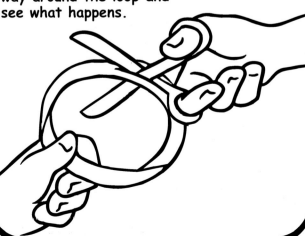

4
Repeat the experiment with a new half-twisted loop of paper, but instead of cutting along the centre of the strip, make your cut about one-third of the way in from one edge of the strip. Keep cutting around the loop and holding your position from the edge until you come back to where you started from. See what happens this time.

© Dr Mark Biddiss 2001, 2005, 2011, Magical Science Book 1 @ www.Dr-Mark.co.uk

WHAT HAPPENS?

You should have first discovered that your half-twisted loop only actually has one continuous flat surface (or one side) and only one continuous long edge - even though it may seem to have two of each!

When you cut the first half-twisted loop lengthways along the centre of the strip, instead of then having two loops as you might expect, amazingly, you will find that you still have only one, but it is now twice as long, twice as thin, has two sides, two edges and has two complete twists in it!

When you cut the second half-twisted loop about one-third of the way in from one edge of the strip, you should end up with two linked loops! Thats one smaller loop with a half-twist (with one side and one edge) linked to a loop twice as big, of about the same width but with two sides, two edges and with two complete twists in it!

SOME QUESTIONS TO THINK ABOUT

1. What do you think is going on? (see 'SO WHAT'S GOING ON?')

2. In step 3 on the previous page you cut the first half-twisted loop lengthways along the centre of the strip and still ended up with a single loop. What happens if you cut this new loop in the same way? (answer provided)

3. In step 4 on the previous page you cut the second half-twisted loop lengthways about one-third in from one edge of the strip and ended up with one small loop linked to one bigger loop. Without disconnecting the two loops, what happens if you then cut the smaller loop lengthways along the centre of the strip, as you did with the loop in step 3? (answer provided)

4. Take a completely fresh strip of paper and make a new half-twisted loop. Instead of cutting the loop lengthways about one-third in from one edge of the strip as you did in step 4, what happens when you cut the loop about one-quarter in from one edge of the strip, or cut even near to, but not on, the centre-line of the strip?

5. What do you discover if you cut in similar ways around loops made with different numbers of twists, such as loops made with one whole twist, or with one-and-a-half twists? (some answers provided)

6. Does the direction of the twists you make in the strip make any difference to the resulting cut loops?

(Numbered answers and explanations to some of the questions are given on the next page)

SO WHAT'S GOING ON?

In steps 1 & 2 on the previous page you made what is known as a Moebius Strip or Moebius Band. This weird one-sided and one-edged loop structure was first described by a German astronomer and mathematician called August Ferdinand Moebius, who died in 1868. I've never been able to find a simple explanation of how and why the Moebius Strip and other twisted loops in this experiment work! The only explanations I've come across seem to involve monstrously and unspeakably complicated numbers, sums and symbols! All I can say is that the weird properties of the Moebius Strip and other loops in this experiment are all due to the twists you make in each loop. If you know of a better explanation than this, please send it to me, cause I'd like to hear it!

© Dr Mark Biddiss 2001, 2005, 2011, Magical Science Book 1 @ www.Dr-Mark.co.uk

WHERE ON EARTH?

Strictly speaking, the Moebius Strip comes from a branch of mathematics called topology. Basically, topology is the study of the properties of deformed structures and surfaces. But although it comes from mathematics, the Moebius Strip can be used in practical scientific ways. All of the scientific applications I know of make use of the fact that the Moebius Strip only actually has one continuous side, which is twice as long as one of the sides on an ordinary untwisted belt of the same size.

Pulley wheels in machines are usually linked and driven by ordinary untwisted, double-sided belts. These belts wear out faster on the inside rubbing or wearing surface (where the pulleys are) than on the outside surface. Because a half-twisted Moebius pulley belt has only one much longer side, it will wear more evenly and last about twice as long. Similarly, a Moebius audio tape loop will record and playback sound for twice as long. Even some modern sculpture has been created around the Moebius Strip design.

And some Space Scientists even compare the shape and continuous properties of the Moebius Strip (and other similarly peculiar topological forms such as the inside surface of a hollow torus or 'ring dough-nut' shape) with the supposed shape of the entire universe! These space scientists reckon that our universe may be so shaped that if you carried on going out into space in a straight line, sooner or later you'd end up back where you started from! Sounds familiar doesn't it!

SOME TRICK TIPS!

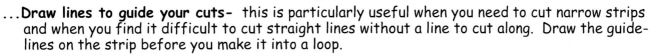

...**Draw lines to guide your cuts-** this is particularly useful when you need to cut narrow strips and when you find it difficult to cut straight lines without a line to cut along. Draw the guide-lines on the strip before you make it into a loop.

...**Use wider paper strips-** good for when you need to cut around a loop more than once and when you find it difficult to cut in straight lines with or without guidelines to cut along.

...**Pinch the loop and snip it on the fold to make a cutting hole** this is useful when you don't want to risk stabbing yourself with your scissors as you pierce them through the paper strip to make a cutting hole.

ANSWERS TO SOME OF THE NUMBERED QUESTIONS:

ANS. 2: If you cut around the loop you got from step 3 earlier, you end up with two linked loops, both the same size as the original but half as wide, each with two sides, two edges and two complete twists in!

ANS. 3: If you cut around the smaller of the two loops from step 4 earlier, you should end up with two loops linked to each other by a double turn in the loop, both the same length, but one about twice as wide as the other, both with two sides and two edges, and each with two twists in!

ANS. 5: An initial loop made with one complete twist (or a 360 degree twist) and cut lengthways along the centre of the strip gives you two linked loops, each also with one complete twist!

ANS. 6: An initial loop made with one-and-a-half-twists (or a 540 degree twist) and cut lengthways along the centre of the strip gives you one loop with a knot in it! Weird or what?

DR MARK'S MAGICAL SCIENCE: BOOK 1 EXPERIMENT NUMBERS

SCIENCE CONTENT	1	2	3	4	5	6	7	8	9	10	11	12	13	14	15	16	17	18	19	20	21	22	23	24
Biology:																								
Life Processes & Living Things																								
Humans (and other animals) as organisms	★	★	★		★	★	★	★	★	★		★	★	★	★			★	★	★	★	★	★	
- Parts of the body		★	★	★		★★						★			★★			★★			★	★★	★	
- Senses			★			★★			★						★★			★★			★	★	★	
- Digestion	★				★					★														
- Movement												★												
- Nervous system		★★	★★									★												
- Reflex response		★★	★																					
- Breathing and respiration																						★★		
Green plants							★★						★★									★★		
- Transport and water							★						★									★		
Living things in their environment														★★					★	★★				
- Adaptation and competition														★★					★★	★★				
Chemistry:	★	★																★				★		
Materials and their Properties																								
Solids, liquids and gases	★	★			★		★	★		★★	★★		★	★		★★	★	★★	★★	★		★		
- Strength, hardness, flexibility, etc.	★			★★★			★★	★★					★	★★	★	★★	★★	★	★			★★		
- Density							★	★			★		★		★	★				★		★		
- Elements, compounds and mixtures				★★			★★						★★	★★		★★	★★					★★		
- Chromatography				★★									★	★		★	★★					★★		
- Condensation																★	★					★★		
- Atomic structure		★								★★			★★						★★			★★		
- Bonding	★★	★								★★			★★									★★		
Changing materials																								
- Temperature and materials	★						★★	★★		★★			★★	★★		★★	★★					★★		
- Physical changes													★★	★★		★	★★					★★		
- Reversible changes										★						★						★★		
- Boiling & evapourating										★				★					★			★★		
- Condensation														★								★		
- Dissolving	★	★								★			★★			★	★					★		
- Non-reversible changes														★			★					★		

© Dr Mark Biddiss 2001, 2005, 2011, Magical Science Book 1 @ www.Dr-Mark.co.uk

	1	2	3	4	5	6	7	8	9	10	11	12	13	14	15	16	17	18	19	20	21	22	23	24
- Burning materials and oxydation	★																							
- Chemical Reactions	★	★												★		★	★							
Rates of reaction																								
- Useful products from organic sources																								
- Polymers and polymerisation																★	★							
- Acics and bases	★									★														
- Energy transfer in reactions	★									★														
Physics:																								
Physical Processes	★	★	★	★	★		★	★	★	★	★	★	★	★		★	★	★		★	★	★		★
Forces and Motion	★★	★★	★★	★★	★★★		★★	★★★		★★	★★	★★	★★	★★		★★	★★		★★	★★★				★★★
- Types of force	★★	★	★★	★	★★		★	★★		★	★	★	★	★		★	★		★	★★		★★		★★
- Pushing and pulling	★★	★	★	★	★		★	★		★	★	★							★	★		★		★
- Gravity	★	★									★													
- Friction and air-resistance					★			★★					★	★★			★			★		★		
- Force and linear motion	★	★	★		★		★	★		★	★	★	★	★		★				★				
- Weight	★★	★										★	★											
- Unbalanced force							★	★		★	★	★	★	★			★			★	★			
- Force and rotation	★	★														★				★				
- Force and pressure	★	★			★			★		★	★	★	★	★			★			★	★			
- Force and acceleration					★					★	★						★			★				
Light and sound																		★		★	★			
- Light and dark					★													★			★			
- Light sources					★★													★				★		★
- Everyday effects of light					★★													★				★		★
- Colour spectrum					★★											★		★		★	★			
- Seeing					★				★									★		★		★		
- Making and detecting sounds													★											
- Hearing								★																
- Vibration and sound										★														
- Waves: amplitude, frequency and wavelength																					★			
- Sound and ultrasound																								
Energy	★	★																						

① EXPLODING WATER

WHAT YOU NEED:
An empty plastic 35mm film can (Kodak or Fuji is good) with the internal sealing snap-on lid, a few effervescent (fizzy) Alka Seltzer-type tablets, water, a tray with sides (to contain the mess!) and preferably some eye protection. Adult supervision is seriously recommended for the under 'teens.

1. Put some water in the empty film pot until it is about one-third full (about 10ml)

2. Drop a fizzy tablet into the water and VERY QUICKLY AND FIRMLY snap on the pot lid – the lid MUST be put on properly!

3. VERY QUICKLY place the pot UPSIDE-DOWN on the tray on a firm, flat surface (like the floor) and stand well back!

Some Questions:
1. What did you notice?
2. What do you think is going on?
3. What other things could you investigate and think about?

© Dr Mark Biddiss 2001, 2005, 2011, Magical Science Book 1 @ www.Dr-Mark.co.u

2. LEVITATING BALLOONS

WHAT YOU NEED:
Three or four rounded balloons, some different-shape balloons and a thick bendy drinking straw (milk-shake type).

1 Bend a thick milk-shake straw into an 'L' shape.

2 Put the long end of the straw between your lips so that the shorter end is pointing straight up, then hold a balloon up just above the end of the straw and STAND VERY STILL.

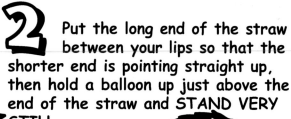

3 While STANDING VERY STILL, blow into the straw and let go of the balloon, and keep on blowing steadily.

4 When you have had a go with one balloon, try a different size balloon.

Some Questions:
1. What did you notice?
2. What do you think is going on?
3. What other things could you investigate and think about?

② FLOATING BALLS

WHAT YOU NEED:
A ping-pong or table-tennis ball and an electric blow hair-dryer.

1. Hold the hairdryer carefully in one hand, pointing the nozzle straight upwards towards the ceiling and switch it on to full power (and be very careful not to pull the electric cable too much at the plug!)

2. Using your other hand, hold the ping-pong ball about 5 to 10cm directly above the hair-dryer nozzle in the upward blowing air-stream.

3. Holding the blowing hair-dryer very still, release the ball in the air-stream and quickly move that hand away.

4. VERY SLOWLY AND CAREFULLY rotate the hair-dryer to point off towards one side instead of straight upwards.

Some Questions:
1. What did you notice?
2. What do you think is going on?
3. What other things could you investigate and think about?

3. LOSING CONTROL

WHAT YOU NEED:
Yourself and perhaps a friend or two - you can easily do this experiment on yourself but it is more fun with a few friends!

1 Stand up straight with your arms folded in front of you. Then lift one of your feet a little off the floor and try to balance steadily on one leg.

2 When you are quite balanced, close your eyes tightly and keep them closed while you try to stay balanced.

Some Questions:
1. What did you notice?
2. What do you think is going on?
3. What other things could you investigate and think about?

© Dr Mark Biddiss 2001, 2005, 2011, Magical Science Book 1 @ www.Dr-Mark.co.uk

④ 'ORRIBLE OOZE

WHAT YOU NEED:
Cornflour (or cornstarch or custard powder), water, mixing bowl, small spoon and some 'orrid green food colouring!

1. Put three heaped teaspoons of cornflour into a mixing bowl and add a few drops of food colouring (optional).

2. Add water to the cornflour, only a spoonful at a time, while stirring and mixing the ooze with your fingers or the spoon. Keep adding water until you get a very thick, oozy, creamy mixture, which feels like a stiff liquid when you are stirring it VERY slowly.

3. See and feel what happens when you tap the surface of the ooze firmly with a finger or the spoon.

4. Pick up a handful of the ooze and squeeze it and roll it around firmly between your hands to make a ball. Then stop rolling and see what happens.

Some Questions:
1. What did you notice?
2. What do you think is going on?
3. What other things could you investigate and think about?

5. SCREAMING STRAWS

WHAT YOU NEED:
A thick drinking straw (milk-shake type), and a pair of scissors.

WARNING! REALLY IRRITATING EXPERIMENT!

1. Flatten one end of a thick drinking straw using your fingers or by sliding it between your front teeth.

2. With some scissors, carefully cut the flattened end of the straw into a slightly blunted point. This makes two pointed, triangular flaps.

Snip here

3. Squeeze the flattened, cut end of the straw between your lips and blow hard.

TIP: If you do not get a sound straight away, try changing how hard you squeeze the straw between your lips and how hard you blow. You may need to change both squeezing and blowing to get a steady sound. It is not always easy so be patient!

Some Questions:
1. What did you notice?
2. What do you think is going on?
3. What other things could you investigate and think about?

© Dr Mark Biddiss 2001, 2005, 2011, Magical Science Book 1 @ www.Dr-Mark.co.uk

⑤ RASPBERRY BALLOONS

WHAT YOU NEED:
A long balloon and a sharp pair of scissors
(be very careful with those sharp scissors!)

1. Using your sharp scissors, very carefully make two cuts near the flattened, closed end of the balloon to form a triangular point. The triangular point should be pointing away from the mouth-piece end of the balloon.

2. Now put the mouth-piece end of the balloon between your lips (as if you were going to blow the balloon up) with the pointed end pointing away from you and blow steadily and firmly (be very careful not to accidentally suck the balloon into your mouth, because you could choke!)

Some Questions:
1. What did you notice?
2. What do you think is going on?
3. What other things could you investigate and think about?

6. PHANTOM PENCILS

WHAT YOU NEED:
Two or more sharpened pencils (though not too sharp!) and a friend. You can do this experiment on yourself but it is not so effective and it's much more fun with a friend anyway!

1. Hold two sharpened pencils side-by-side. Make sure their pointed ends are lined up.

2. Ask a friend to hold out one of their arms with the palm of their hand facing upwards. Ask them to roll up any sleeve to their elbow and to close their eyes tightly. Tell them to keep VERY STILL.

3. GENTLY press the two pencil points against one of your friend's fingertips and ask them how many points they can feel. Try this again on two or three of their other fingertips.

4. Now do the same thing on several different places on their bare arms.

TIP: Your friend will find it easier to keep their arm still if you get them to rest it against a steady surface, such as on a tabletop.

Some Questions:
1. What did you notice?
2. What do you think is going on?
3. What other things could you investigate and think about?

⑦ BLACK MAGIC

WHAT YOU NEED:
A black felt-tip marker pen (non-permanent or water-based ink and NOT permanent ink), dry white blotting-paper (or coffee filter paper), water, a clothes washing-line peg (or paperclip) and a cup (preferably see-through).

1. Pour some water in a cup, about 1cm deep.

2. Cut a dry piece of white blotting-paper (or coffee filter paper) into a strip about 2- or 3cm wide and long enough to hang down the inside of the cup, from the top edge to the bottom.

3. With a black felt-tip marker pen, draw a small black round spot, about 3 or 4mm in size and about 2cm from one end of the paper strip. Instead of a round dot you could draw a thick line (about 2mm wide) across the width of the strip and about 2cm from one end.

4. Carefully lower the blotting-paper strip down the inside of the cup until it trails into the water. Fix the strip in place with the peg or paper-clip to the top rim of the cup, making sure that the black spot or line is just a few millimetres ABOVE the surface level of the water. Now watch for five to ten minutes.

Some Questions:
1. What did you notice?
2. What do you think is going on?
3. What other things could you investigate and think about?

⑦ SECRET COLOURS

WHAT YOU NEED:
Five or six sugar coated candy-sweets all of the SAME colour (purple, brown, black and/or green work well) and/or some liquid food colouring dye (black and/or green are good), a cup (preferably see-through), dry white blotting-paper (coffee filter paper is good), a washing-line clothes peg (or paper-clip) and some warm water.

1. Put a few of the same colour candy-sweets into the cup and then pour in some warm water. You only really need just enough water to wet the candy-sweets and to be able to stir them around to help dissolve and wash off the coloured pigment in the sugar coating into the water. So you should end up with coloured water.

2. Cut out a strip of the white blotting-paper (or coffee filter paper) about 2 or 3cm wide and long enough to hang down the inside of the cup, from the top edge to the bottom.

3. Carefully lower the blotting-paper strip down the inside of the cup until it trails into the coloured water and fix it in place with your peg or paper-clip around the top rim of the cup.
Now watch for five to ten minutes.

4. Repeat the above but use the liquid food colouring dye instead of the warm water and colour candy-sweets

Some Questions:
1. What did you notice?
2. What do you think is going on?
3. What other things could you investigate and think about?

© Dr Mark Biddiss 2001, 2005, 2011, Magical Science Book 1 @ www.Dr-Mark.co.uk

8. DIVING PEN-TOPS

WHAT YOU NEED: A plastic (preferably see-through) pen-top with pocket-clip, an empty see-through plastic bottle with the screw-on cap, some modelling clay, a tall drinking-glass, measuring jug or bowl and some water.

1. If your pen-top has a small air-hole at the narrow end, you will need to completely block this off with a small piece of modelling clay or putty. Blocking it off with a small ball of putty from the inside works well (push the putty up inside!). Then fix some modelling putty around the pocket-clip of the pen-top, making sure NOT to completely block up the entrance hole where the pen would slide in.

Block hole if needed

2. Initially, you need to fix enough modelling clay to weight the pen-top so that it only just floats (pocket-clip and wide open end downwards) and is just on the point of sinking. Try it in a tall drinking glass, measuring jug or bowl full of water until you get it just right.

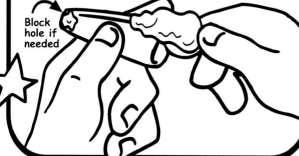

3. Completely fill your plastic bottle with water, carefully lower your correctly weighted pen-top into the plastic bottle and carefully screw the bottle cap on tightly.

4. Squeeze the plastic bottle quite hard with both hands, hold for a few seconds and then release your squeeze.

Some Questions:
1. What did you notice?
2. What do you think is going on?
3. What other things could you investigate and think about?

© Dr Mark Biddiss 2001, 2005, 2011, Magical Science Book 1 @ www.Dr-Mark.co.uk

⑧ SAUCY SINKER

WHAT YOU NEED:
A plastic sachet of ketchup sauce (or vinegar) that floats (from your local restaurant), some metal paper-clips, the kitchen sink or bowl, an empty see-through plastic bottle with the screw-on cap and some water.

1. Float the plastic sachet of sauce (or vinegar) in a sink or bowl of water. You need to adjust it so that it only just floats. Carefully fix one or more paper-clips to the plastic sachet if it floats too easily, but not too many clips to make it sink. And be careful not to puncture a hole in your sachet with the clips.

2. Completely fill the plastic bottle with water, then carefully push the plastic sachet into the top and then carefully screw the bottle cap on tightly. You should see the sachet of sauce floating at the top of the bottle.

3. Squeeze the sides of the plastic bottle as hard as you can, hold for a few seconds and then release your squeeze.

Some Questions:
1. What did you notice?
2. What do you think is going on?
3. What other things could you investigate and think about?

BAG BOMBS

WHAT YOU NEED:
Baking soda (or bicarbonate of soda or bicarb), vinegar, water (preferably warm), paper towel or tissue, see-through zip-lock plastic bag (they're the ones you can seal up and make air-tight), large spoon and measuring jug or cup.

WARNING: VERY SMELLY EXPERIMENT!

1. Test your zip-lock bag for leaks by filling it with water, close it up, tip it upside-down and give it a gentle squeeze. If no water leaks out, it should work just fine. If it leaks, try another one.

Wrap about 1½ tablespoons of baking soda in a square of paper towel or tissue.

2. Pour into your plastic bag about a quarter of a cup (about 50ml) of water (preferably warm) and about half a cup (about 100ml) of vinegar.

3. Zip-close your bag about halfway, carefully put your baking soda packet into the bag and then fully zip-close the bag as quickly as possible.

4. Give the bag a good shake, quickly put it in the sink, bath or on the ground outside and stand well back!

Some Questions:
1. What did you notice?
2. What do you think is going on?
3. What other things could you investigate and think about?

© Dr Mark Biddiss 2001, 2005, 2011, Magical Science Book 1 @ www.Dr-Mark.co.uk

10 SELF-INFLATING BALLOONS ★

WHAT YOU NEED:
A balloon, small funnel, a small bottle with a narrow neck opening (to fit the balloon on), baking soda powder (or bicarbonate of soda, or bicarb) and some vinegar. How much powder and vinegar you need will depend on the sizes of the bottle and balloon you use; you'll find out!

WARNING: VERY SMELLY EXPERIMENT!

1 Pour some vinegar into the small bottle, say, about one-third full to start.

2 Push your funnel into the opening of the balloon and pour in some baking soda until the balloon is, say, about half-full to start.

HALF

3 Carefully stretch the mouth of the balloon over the neck of the bottle, making sure it fits tightly. At the same time make sure the rest of the balloon containing the powder hangs down the side of the bottle so that no powder can fall out; it help too here if you can put a few twists in the balloon just above the level of the powder.

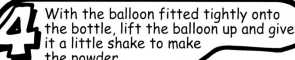

4 With the balloon fitted tightly onto the bottle, lift the balloon up and give it a little shake to make the powder fall out and into the vinegar.

Some Questions:
1. What did you notice?
2. What do you think is going on?
3. What other things could you investigate and think about?

OBEDIENT ★ SQUIRTY BOTTLE

WHAT YOU NEED:
An empty plastic fizzy-drink bottle (up to 1 litre) with the screw-on cap, a very thin pin (or nail) and some pliers.

WANTED GROWN-UP HELP

1. WITH A GROWN-UP'S HELP grip the back end of your thin pin (or nail) with the pliers and firmly but CAREFULLY use the point of the pin to pierce three or four tiny holes around the bottom of the plastic bottle.

2. Stand the bottle and hold it firmly in some shallow water in a bowl or the sink, making sure the water is deep enough to be above the holes you just made. While still standing the bottle in the bowl or sink, fill it to the top with water.

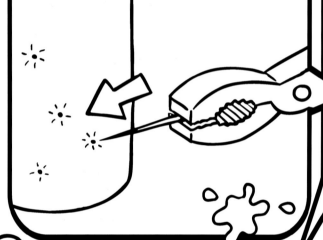

3. Holding the bottle near the neck opening, slowly lift it up above the water and hold it there steady for a few seconds.

4. While still holding the bottle steadily above the water, use your other hand to carefully screw on the cap tightly.

Some Questions:
1. What did you notice?
2. What do you think is going on?
3. What other things could you investigate and think about?

⑫ MAGNETIC HANDS

WHAT YOU NEED:
A friend who is at least as strong as you are in their arms and shoulders. (These experiments can be done on your own but they're easier to do if you can find a friend to help).

1. Face your friend and keeping your elbows tucked in against the sides of your body, hold your hands straight out in front as if you're about to start clapping. You need your arms to be bent in an L-shape at your elbows and the palms of your hands facing each other. You should start with your hands about 15 to 20cm apart. Ask your friend to face you with their hands and arms in the same position.

2. Get them to stand close enough so that they can rest their palms against the back of your hands. The back of your right hand should be touching the palm of their left hand and the back of your left hand should be touching the palm of their right hand. With all hands in place, you need to push outwards against your friends hands as hard as you can and they must try hard to push inwards to stop your hands from moving. Remember to keep your elbows tucked in at your sides at all times. Continue this hard pushing without resting for an instant for about one minute if you can, or otherwise for as long as possible.

3. After about one minute or when you just can't push hard any longer, both you and your friend must stop pushing altogether and RELAX your arm muscles, and ask your friend to take their hands from yours. Now VERY GENTLY AND SLOWLY swing your hands together, back and forth as if clapping in slow motion.

Some Questions:
1. What did you notice?
2. What do you think is going on?
3. What other things could you investigate and think about?

★ FIRE-RAISING ★

WHAT YOU NEED:
Small candle (preferably one that can float - night-light candles are good), a bowl (at least 2 or 3cm deep and preferably see-through), see-through glass jar or beaker (the narrower the better), water, modeling clay or putty and matches (or lighter).

1. Stick three or four small blobs of modelling putty around the rim edge of your glass jar. (The blobs of putty need to be secured and evenly spaced around the rim so that they can support and hold the rim of the upturned jar just one or two millimetres up off the bottom of the bowl.)

2. At least half-fill the bowl with water.

DANGER GROWN-UP HELP NEEDED

3. Gently place your candle so that it floats in the centre of the bowl of water (see 'SOME TRICK TIPS' for a suggestion on how to fix a candle that doesn't float).

4. Ask a grown-up to light the candle with a match (or lighter) and then gently lower the upturned jar down over the burning candle and down into the water, so that the rim of the jar is well below the surface of the water and comes to rest on the bottom of the bowl on the blobs of putty you placed around the rim.

Some Questions:
1. What did you notice?
2. What do you think is going on?
3. What other things could you investigate and think about?

© Dr Mark Biddiss 2001, 2005, 2011, Magical Science Book 1 @ www.Dr-Mark.co.uk

★ SUCKING GLASSES ★

(13)

WHAT YOU NEED:
A drinking glass, some plasticine modelling clay, a flat dinner plate or wide tea-plate, some cold water and some very hot water (but not too hot to burn you).

DANGER GROWN-UP HELP NEEDED

1. Stick three or four small blobs of modelling clay spaced evenly around the rim edge of the glass.

2. Completely cover the glass with very hot water in the sink or washing-up bowl.

3. Leaving the glass in the hot water for a few minutes, put some cold water into the plate, at least about 1cm deep.

4. After a few minutes remove the glass from the hot water and quickly make sure the modelling clay blobs are still in place. Then very quickly turn the glass upside-down and place it onto the plate of cold water. Make sure that the level of the cold water in the plate is at least ½ cm above the rim edge of the upturned glass. Now leave the glass resting in the plate for, say, about 30 minutes and see what happens.

Some Questions:
1. What did you notice?
2. What do you think is going on?
3. What other things could you investigate and think about?

(14) MYSTERY OF THE MOVING EGG EGGSPERIMENT

WHAT YOU NEED:
To eggsperience and eggsamine this eggstraodinary eggsperiment you'll need a raw egg, a cooked hard-boiled egg and a broad flat, smooth surface (such as a large table top or smooth floor or even a dinner plate). (And I'll try to resist any more egg wordplay jokes OK!).

1. Take a raw egg and set it spinning quite fast on its side on the flat smooth surface.

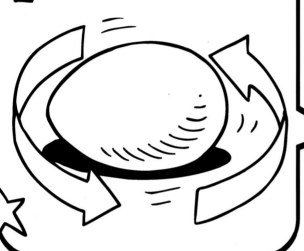

2. Press down on the spinning egg lightly with your fingers, but firmly enough to stop it spinning.

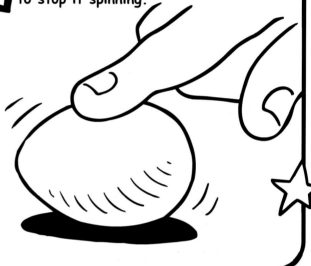

3. As soon as the egg stops spinning, IMMEDIATELTY lift your fingers away.

Some Questions:
1. What did you notice?
2. What do you think is going on?
3. What other things could you investigate and think about?

15. TASTELESS TONGUE

WHAT YOU NEED:
Firstly, you will need at least three or four of the following raw foods: an apple, a potato, a carrot, a turnip, a pear and an onion (and make sure that they are all fresh, juicy and crisp). You will also need some plates, a sharp knife (or grater), some spoons or forks, a cup of drinking water and a friend.

1. Cut (or grate) some apple, potato, carrot, turnip and some pear (or at least three of these food items) into small pieces of about the same size. Clean your knife or grater each time you go to cut a different food item. Place each food separately on its own plate and with its own spoon or fork.

2. Close your eyes, squeeze and block your nostrils tightly closed (you should not be able to smell anything or breath through your nose), and ask your friend to feed you just a little of one of the foods without telling you which one it is.

3. Chew it for just a few seconds and try to taste which of the foods you are eating. Swallow it or spit it out.

Rinse your mouth with water, and ask your friend to feed you a different food. Repeat this until you have tasted all the foods

Some Questions:
1. What did you notice?
2. What do you think is going on?
3. What other things could you investigate and think about?

© Dr Mark Biddiss 2001, 2005, 2011, Magical Science Book 1 @ www.Dr-Mark.co.uk

15. APPLE-POTATOES & ONION-APPLES

WHAT YOU NEED:
An apple, a raw potato and an onion. You'll also need a sharp enough knife to cut the apple, potato and onion into smaller 'bite-size' pieces.

WARNING: GROWN-UP HELP NEEDED WITH SHARP KNIFE!

1. Carefully cut at least two or three bit-size pieces each off of the apple, the potato and the onion. Clean your knife just before you cut each different food item. Place each food item on its own plate, nowhere near the other two.

2. Picking up the potato in one hand and the apple in the other, slowly chew a juicy piece of raw potato for 5 or 10 seconds, while at the same time strongly sniffing a juicy piece of fresh apple. Maybe too try it the other way around: slowly chew a juicy piece of fresh apple while strongly sniffing a juicy piece of raw potato.

3. Wash your hands, rinse your mouth out a few times with some water and breathe deeply a few times through your nose (with no apple, potato or anything else in the way) to clear your nasal air-ways.

4. Now picking up the apple in one hand and the onion in the other, slowly chew a juicy piece of fresh apple while at the same time strongly sniffing a juicy piece of fresh onion. Maybe too try it the other way around: chew a juicy piece of fresh onion while strongly sniffing a juicy piece of fresh apple.

Some Questions:
1. What did you notice?
2. What do you think is going on?
3. What other things could you investigate and think about?

16. BOUNCIN BLUBBER BALLS

WHAT YOU NEED:
Some water soluble (or washable) white PVA glue, borax powder (a natural general-purpose household cleaner), some water, a measuring jug, a large spoon (or tablespoon), and some food dye (optional). You might also want to put down some old newspaper or plastic to protect your work surfaces.

1. Put 1 heaped tablespoon of borax powder into a measuring jug and add about 300ml of water. Stir well for a few seconds to dissolve the borax powder into the water and until it looks white and cloudy. Leave this to stand still for a few minutes until the water clears and you should see some un-dissolved borax powder in the bottom of the jug.

2. Now pour about 2 tablespoons of white PVA glue slowly into the borax-water mixture. A stringy glob of white plastic material will immediately form floating in the borax solution.

3. Quickly reach into the jug and lift out as much of the glob as you can. It will feel very, very, stringy, gooey, soft and slippery! This will get less so as you handle it. Gently squeeze, slide and roll the glob from one hand to the other try not to fold it. You may find it less slippery to hold and move around if you wash the glob and your hands under tap water once or twice while you roll it around from hand to hand. Also, stopping briefly to dry your hands and then continuing with the rolling can also help to dry the glob a little and make it easier to handle. Keep rolling for a few minutes until the glob holds as a ball.

4. Now gently throw your white blubbery ball onto a hard, smooth, flat surface (such as wall, floor or table-top) and see what happens. Then perhaps throw it harder.

WARNING: MESSY EXPERIMENT & DONT EAT THE MATERIALS (THEY ARE NOT POISONOUS BUT COULD STILL BE HARMFUL)

Some Questions:
1. What did you notice?
2. What do you think is going on?
3. What other things could you investigate and think about?

⑰ BALLOON KEBABS

WHAT YOU NEED:
A few round balloons, a sharp tooth-pick, cocktail stick and/or sharp wooden/bamboo barbeque skewer sticks and a little cooking oil or washing-up liquid detergent (or other liquid lubricant).

1. Inflate a balloon as fully as possible, hold it inflated for a minute or so, and then let it deflate and go down flat again. Fully inflate it a second time and then let it deflate until it is about half or two-thirds full of air. Tie a knot in the mouth end of the balloon to stop it deflating any more.

2. Dip the sharp pointed tip of a toothpick (or cocktail stick) in some cooking oil and push it very gently against the darker area of rubber opposite the tied end of the balloon.

3. Spin the toothpick by rotating it back and forth between your fingers. At the same time, very gently and slowly begin to push the spinning toothpick into the balloon. Keep on pushing and spinning until the pointed tip of the toothpick pierces through the balloons surface.

4. If you're using a long-enough stick, see if you can push the stick right through the balloon and out the other side through the darker area of rubber immediately surrounding the knot.

Some Questions:
1. What did you notice?
2. What do you think is going on?
3. What other things could you investigate and think about?

17. MORE BALLOON KEBABS

WHAT YOU NEED: A few round balloons, sharp toothpicks, cocktail-sticks or sharp wooden barbeque skewer sticks.

1. Inflate a balloon as fully as possible, hold it inflated for a minute or so, and then let it deflate and go down flat again. Fully inflate it a second time and then let it deflate until it is about half or two-thirds full of air. Tie a knot in the mouth end of the balloon to stop it deflating any more.

2. Carefully hold your stick and push the sharp point very gently against the darker area of rubber surrounding the knot, as close as possible to the knot.

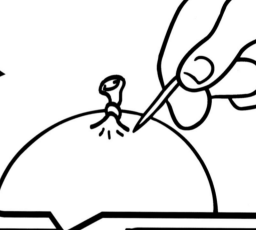

3. Spin the stick by rotating it back and forth between your fingers. At the same time, very gently and slowly begin to push the spinning stick into the balloon. Keep on pushing and spinning until the pointed tip of the stick pierces through the balloon's surface, next to the knot.

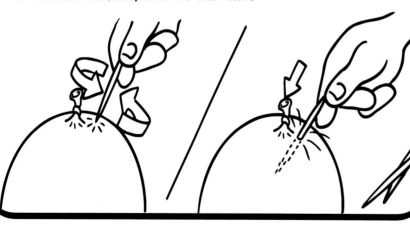

4. If you're using a long enough stick, see if you can push the stick right through the balloon and out the other side through the darker area of rubber opposite the knotted end of the balloon.

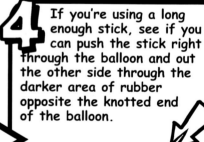

Some Questions:
1. What did you notice?
2. What do you think is going on?
3. What other things could you investigate and think about?

17 WATER-BAG PORCUPINES

WHAT YOU NEED:
A polythene plastic freezer or sandwich bag, a sharp toothpick, cocktail-stick, sharp pencil and/or a sharp wooden bamboo barbeque skewer stick.

1. About half fill the plastic bag with water and then in one hand hold it firmly by the top open edges.

2. Using one of your sharp sticks in the otherhand, slowly but firmly twist and push the point of the stick through the plastic bag below the water-line, as if you wanted to make a hole for the water to pour through. Stop pushing once the point of the stick is well inside the plastic bag and let go of the stick.

3. If your stick is long enough, such as with the pencil or bamboo skewer, now try to push the stick right the way through the plastic bag and out the other side. Again, stop pushing once the point of the stick is sticking right out from the other side of the plastic bag.

4. Now slowly pull the stick bag through the bag and completely remove it from the holes you've made.

Some Questions:
1. What did you notice?
2. What do you think is going on?
3. What other things could you investigate and think about?

© Dr Mark Biddiss 2001, 2005, 2011, Magical Science Book 1 @ www.Dr-Mark.co.uk

18. WHITE GHOSTS

1 Hold this book at arms length in front of you with a bright light shining on this page (such as in bright daylight or under a desk lamp) and stare hard into the white mouth of the ghostly black figure below for about 30 seconds. Make sure that you stare at the same place in the centre of the ghost for the whole time.

2 After 30 seconds of staring at the ghostly figure, immediately switch your stare into the spooky graveyard ruin scene below.

Some Questions:
1. What did you notice?
2. What do you think is going on?
3. What other things could you investigate and think about?

18. SPECTRAL SPECTRES

WHAT YOU NEED: Some assorted felt or marker colouring pens (preferably including bright blue, red, green and perhaps also yellow, magenta/bright pink/crimson and cyan/greenish-blue/turquoise), some copies of this worksheet (maybe the same number of sheets as the number of different colour pens you have) and a bright light source (bright day or sunlight or a desk lamp).

1. Choose one of your bright colouring pens to completely colour in the ghostly outline below. Maybe use a different colour for the eyes and mouth. Then hold this sheet out in front of you at arms length with a bright light shining upon it (such as in bright day light or a desk lamp) and stare hard into the mouth of the ghostly figure for at least 30 seconds. Make sure that you stare at the same place in the mouth of the ghost for the whole time.

2. After 30 seconds or so of staring at the ghostly figure (the longer the better), immediately switch your stare into the middle of the spooky graveyard scene below and blink quickly.

Some Questions:
1. What did you notice?
2. What do you think is going on?
3. What other things could you investigate and think about?

SOAPY SPEED BOATS

WHAT YOU NEED: Washing up liquid (or other liquid detergent), a bowel or sink of water (make sure that whatever container you use is very clean with no traces of soap or detergent anywhere otherwise the experiments won't work), a pencil, a small piece of cardboard and a pair of scissors.

1. Cut your small piece of cardboard into a boat-shape. Start with a rectangle-shape piece of card about 5 or 6cm long and about 2 or 3cm wide. Cut it to be pointed at one end for the front of the boat (the bow) and along the back edge (the stern) cut out a small triangle-shaped hole. If you don't cut the triangle of card out completely, you can bend it upwards and use it as a handle.

2. Gripping the triangle-shaped handle, VERY GENTLY rest your boat on the surface of the water in your bowl or sink.

3. Dip the pointed end of your pencil in some washing-up liquid and then hold the pencil-point just over the triangle-shaped hole in the stern of your boat. Wait for a drop of washing-up liquid to fall into the gap or quickly and gently touch the surface of the water within the triangle-shape hole.

Some Questions:
1. What did you notice?
2. What do you think is going on?
3. What other things could you investigate and think about?

FLOATING METAL

WHAT YOU NEED:
A small sewing-needle, a little cooking-oil, a small piece of paper tissue, two forks, a deep plate, bowl, frying pan or sink (make sure whatever you use is completely clean with no traces of detergent or soap) and some clean water.

1. Put some water into your deep plate, bowl, frying pan or sink, at least 2cm deep.

2. Wipe a very thin layer of cooking oil onto your needle and rest it on a small dry square of paper tissue (about 3cm x 3cm)

3. Very gently float the tissue and needle onto the surface of the water

4. Using the prongs of your two forks, VERY GENTLY AND SLOWLY push down on the floating tissue paper on each side of the needle to sink the tissue down into the water.

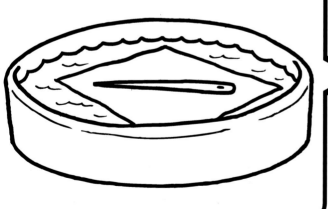

Some Questions:
1. What did you notice?
2. What do you think is going on?
3. What other things could you investigate and think about?

19. SCARY FINGER & PETRIFIED PEPPER

WHAT YOU NEED:
Some finely-ground pepper, a clean dinner plate or large frying pan (make sure the plate or pan is completely clean with no traces of detergent or soap), clean water and some washing-up liquid (or other detergent)

1. Put some water into your dinner plate or frying pan, at least ½ cm deep.

2. Lightly sprinkle a small amount of the finely ground pepper all over the surface of the water and leave it for a few seconds to settle and spread out evenly.

3. Put a small amount of washing-up liquid or detergent onto the end of a finger

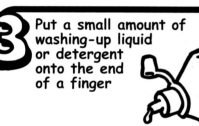

4. Very lightly and gently dip the detergent-coated finger into the floating pepper in the middle of the plate or pan.

Some Questions:
1. What did you notice?
2. What do you think is going on?
3. What other things could you investigate and think about?

© Dr Mark Biddiss 2001, 2005, 2011, Magical Science Book 1 @ www.Dr-Mark.

WATER CIRCLES

WHAT YOU NEED:
About 12 to 15cm of very thin sewing-thread, a clean dinner plate or large frying pan (make sure the plate or pan is completely clean with no traces of detergent or soap), clean water and some washing-up liquid (or other detergent)

1 Put some water into your dinner plate or frying pan, at least 1/2 cm deep.

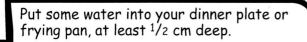

2 Tie your sewing-thread into a small knotted loop and very gently float it onto the surface of the water

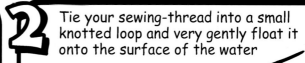

3 Put a small amount of washing-up liquid or detergent onto the end of a finger

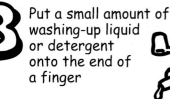

4 Very lightly and gently dip the detergent-coated finger into the surface of the water inside the floating loop.

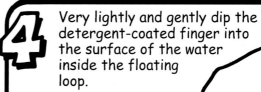

Some Questions:
1. What did you notice?
2. What do you think is going on?
3. What other things could you investigate and think about?

20. FLYING FLIPPING FISH

WHAT YOU NEED: Some paper, a ruler, some scissors and a pencil or pen.

1. Cut a strip of paper somewhere between 20 to 30cm long and 2 to 3cm wide. Note your measurements.

2. Make a cut exactly halfway across the width of the strip, about 3 or 4cm from one end. Turn the strip around and do the same thing the other end. Make sure that your two cuts come from opposite sides of the strip towards the centre, one cut from one long edge and one from the opposite long edge.

3. Bend the strip in the middle, bring the two ends together and form a closed loop by sliding the cut slot at one end into the slot at the other end. You should end up with something that looks like a round-nosed fish.

4. Grip the paper fish by one side (not by the nose or tail) and hold it so that the fish looks like its swimming on its side and towards your right. Then lift it high above your head in this swimming position and drop it.

Some Questions:
1. What did you notice?
2. What do you think is going on?
3. What other things could you investigate and think about?

COLOUR-NAMES & NAMING-COLOURS

WHAT YOU NEED:
One or two sheets of white paper (you'll be writing words so lined paper might be better for you), a selection of different colour bright marker pens or crayons (have at least four different colours if you can and only use yellow if it's easy to read). You also need a grown-up and perhaps a very young child just able to read and make sure nobody is colour-blind!).

1. Using your colour pens, you need to copy out the following two lists of words (best in capital letters) into two columns onto a sheet of white paper. Use a different colour to write each word. To make things more interesting, I suggest that you use your black, blue and brown marker pens to write the words BLACK, BLUE and BROWN. But it's important to make sure that you DON'T write any of the colour names with a marker pen of that same colour. For example, don't write the word BLUE with the blue marker, or the word RED with the red marker. Also, DON'T use the same colour marker pen to write words that are next to each other, one above the other. I suggest leaving a gap of at least two or three words before you use the same colour marker again to write another word. So, here's your two lists of words to copy out:

BUS	RED
MUM	GREEN
TABLE	BLUE
CAT	YELLOW
GIRL	BLACK
BALL	BROWN
CAR	YELLOW
DOOR	BLUE
TOY	RED
DAD	BROWN
HOUSE	BLACK
BOY	GREEN

2. Read both lists of words out loud as quickly as you reasonably can (certainly don't take longer than you need);

3. Now go through the lists again but this time DON'T read the words. Instead look at each word and say out loud what colour it's written in. Again, go through the list as quickly as you can.

4. Now give the list to someone of a very different age to you and ask them to repeat what you just did. The idea is to see if there is any difference between the ways a grown-up goes through the lists and the way a young child goes through the lists.

Some Questions:
1. What did you notice?
2. What do you think is going on?
3. What other things could you investigate and think about?

22 ★ CRUSHING CANS ★

WHAT YOU NEED:
A baking tray or bowl full of chilled or ice-cold water, a tablespoon, a little more water (preferably hot), one or more empty ring-pull aluminium soft drink cans, a cooking stove burner or hot-plate (adult help wanted especially here), some heat-proof tongs or a good oven mitt with thumb to securely hold the can (you could make some tongs out of a wire clothes hanger).

1 Place your tray or bowl of chilled water on a work surface as near as you can to your cooking stove;

2 Then add a tablespoon or so of water (preferably hot) to an empty ring-pull aluminium soft-drink can, just enough to cover the bottom inside. Using hot water will help speed things up a little.

WANTED GROWN-UP HELP

3 With an adult's help, heat the can (with water inside) on the stove burner or hotplate until the water boils. When you see plenty of so-called steam coming from the can, let the water boil vigorously for one more minute. (By the way, what most people call steam is really condensed water vapour, steam is actually invisible. Also, NEVER EVER HEAT A SEALED OR CLOSED METAL CAN.)

4 After one minute, grip the can near the bottom carefully and securely with the tongs or oven mitt, as near to the heat as possible. Now brace yourself, and in one swift movement, quickly lift the can off the stove, turn the can over and place it upside-down in the chilled water in the tray or bowl. You must be swift with this last step, maybe practice it a few times first before you do the real experiment.

★ AND DON'T FORGET TO TURN THE STOVE OFF **AT THE END EITHER**!

Some Questions:
1. What did you notice?
2. What do you think is going on?
3. What other things could you investigate and think about?

22. GHOSTLY SHRINKING BOTTLES

WHAT YOU NEED:
An empty 1 - 2 litre plastic bottle with the screw-on cap, an electric blow-hair dryer.

1. Screw the cap onto the empty plastic bottle but only very loosely at this time; you should be able to easily squeeze the bottle to force air out through the loosely fitted cap.

2. Switch on the blow hair-dryer to one of its hottest settings and use it to heat the bottle all over for at least 30 seconds.

3. When you've finished heating the bottle, quickly screw the cap on tightly and wait patiently for at least a few minutes.

+ WAIT

Some Questions:
1. What did you notice?
2. What do you think is going on?
3. What other things could you investigate and think about?

23. UNREADABLE WORDS & INVISIBLE LETTERS

1 As quickly as you can read out loud the phrases in the two triangles below.

Watch out for deliberate mistakes!

Triangle 1:
I
LOVE
PARIS IN THE
THE SPRINGTIME

Triangle 2:
A
BIRD
IN THE
THE HAND

2 Read them both through out loud again, but this time look at the words more closely and read more slowly.

3 Now go through the sentence below quickly and just once, and count how many times the letter F appears:

FINISHED FILES ARE THE RE-SULT OF YEARS OF SCIENTIF-IC STUDY COMBINED WITH THE EXPERIENCE OF MANY YEARS

4 Now give the book to someone of a very different age to you and ask them to repeat what you just did.

Some Questions:
1. What did you notice?
2. What do you think is going on?
3. What other things could you investigate and think about?

24. VANISHING RINGS & LINKING LOOPS

WHAT YOU NEED:
Several strips of paper about 30cm long (any longer is OK) and about 3cm wide, a pair of round-nosed safety scissors, some sticky-tape and a pencil or pen (optional).

1 Take a strip of paper and bend it around to make a loop or band, overlapping the ends of the strip by about 1cm.

2 Take hold of one of the overlapping ends, twist or turn it over half a turn (through 180 degrees) and then place it back overlapping the other end again. Then use sticky tape to stick the overlapping ends together. You should now have a loop or band with a half-twist in it.

3 Using the scissors, CAREFULLY cut the loop length-ways along the centre of the strip, as if trying to cut it into two separate thinner loops. Cut right the way around the loop and see what happens.

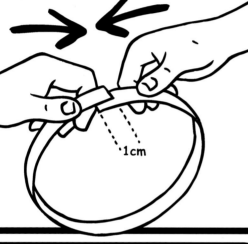

4 Repeat the experiment with a new half-twisted loop of paper, but instead of cutting along the centre of the strip, make your cut about one-third of the way in from one edge of the strip. Keep cutting around the loop and holding your position from the edge until you come back to where you started from. See what happens this time.

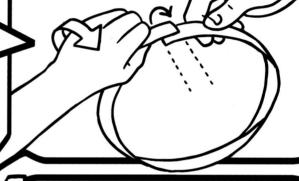

Some Questions:
1. What did you notice?
2. What do you think is going on?
3. What other things could you investigate and think about?

NOTES

NOTES